ADVANCES IN HEALTH MANAGEMENT

Edited by **Ubaldo Comite**

Advances in Health Management
http://dx.doi.org/10.5772/65535
Edited by Ubaldo Comite

Contributors

Aida Isabel Tavares, Alicia De La Pena, Bernardo Amezcua, Beata Gavurova, Tatiana Vagasova, Mohd Idzwan Mohd Salleh, Rosni Abdullah, Nasriah Zakaria, Pietro Iaquinta, Justyna Kujawska, Tullio Romita, Antonella Perri, Muhiuddin Haider

Published by InTech

Janeza Trdine 9, 51000 Rijeka, Croatia

Publishing Process Manager Iva Simcic
Technical Editor SPi Global
Cover InTech Design team

First published August, 2017
Printed in Croatia
Legal deposit, Croatia: National and University Library in Zagreb

Additional hard copies can be obtained from orders@intechopen.com

Advances in Health Management, Edited by Ubaldo Comite
p. cm.
Print ISBN 978-953-51-3437-4
Online ISBN 978-953-51-3438-1

For EU product safety concerns:
IN TECH d.o.o., Prolaz Marije Krucifikse Kozulić 3, 51000 Rijeka, Croatia,
info@intechopen.com or visit our website at intechopen.com.

Meet the editor

Ubaldo Comite was born in Cosenza, Italy, on June 14, 1971. He has a degree in Law (1994) and Economics (1996) at the University of Messina (Italy) and earned his PhD degree in Public Administration at the University of Calabria (Italy), in 2005. Currently, he is a professor of Health Management, Budget and Business Organization at the University of Calabria. Furthermore, he is a professor of Business Administration at the University "Giustino Fortunato" (Italy). He has authored several book chapters and over 60 peer-reviewed journals/proceeding papers. He served as an International Program Committee member for several conferences. His research interests are private and public management, nonprofit organizations and accounting, and health management.

Contents

Preface

The production of healthcare services had been out of the business, organizational, and technological dynamics that continually revolutionized the production of all other goods and services for a long time. Nowadays, this marginality has ceased as the need for healthcare is rising. Healthcare is now at the center of attention influenced by the never-ending demand of medical technology and substantial resource scarcity that imposes substantial organizational and entrepreneurial innovations. One decisive challenge that has emerged from such a situation is the management of healthcare processes, in the broad sense: healthcare professionals are called upon to demonstrate their ability to cope with complex problems because they are characterized in an institutional, ethical, organizational, and economic sense.

The book makes it possible to realize the specific nature of the problem. Its multidimensionality and the original approach are contributed and harmonized by scholars belonging to different disciplines.

This book contains eight chapters in a single segment (*Health Management*), which, throughout the author's different approaches to the subject, help us to understand the issues of the health sector.

Chapter 1 "Low-Cost Health/Medical Tourism of Italians" addresses the theme of the so-called medical tourism or health tourism. The authors try to show how travel for touristic reasons can be matched to travel for reasons of health or well-being.

Chapter 2 "The Future Population of the Industrialized Countries" is devoted to the problem of the inexorable decline of the more developed countries with respect to the population. Aging is reaching intolerable levels on economy, both from the active point of view (available workers) and the passive point of view (e.g., health costs, pensions), redesigning a worrying scenario for the near future.

Chapter 3 "Extending Health Information System Evaluation with an Importance-Performance Map Analysis" shows how the evaluation of a health information system is a necessary task for the determination of the effective use of the system and how it enhances the productivity of medical practitioners. The chapter also provides a valuable recommendation for the policy and decision-makers at the managerial level on how to apply the proposed system evaluation method of a health information system in producing more efficient strategic planning for further system upgrades and new implementation at health facilities.

Chapter 4 "European Health System Typologies: Last 30 Years Under Review" is devoted to the classification of national health systems into homogeneous groups. The last 30 years are divided into two periods (1985–2000 and 2000–2015) in order to present and briefly describe most influential national health system typologies.

In Chapter 5 "Assessment of Avoidable Mortality Concepts in the European Union Countries, Their Benefits and Limitations," the authors compare the impact of four lists of causes of death on the age-standardized amenable death rates across the European Union countries in 2014 by using statistical methods. They conclude that the structure of diseases and the age limits influence the value of standardized amenable death rates and hence it is useful to develop the concept of amenable mortality at the national level in the light of actual availability of medical skills and effective treatments in the country.

In Chapter 6 "The Efficiency of Post-Communist Countries' Health Systems," the authors demonstrate the study of the health systems in 28 post-communist countries of the former Eastern bloc in order to determine the efficiency of the analyzed systems. The used method is the so-called method of data envelopment analysis (DEA). Recommendations are formulated, and projections are presented for the inefficient countries, that is, those countries that were in the Soviet sphere of influence after the Second World War, so that they can achieve such health results as in the case of the most developed European countries.

Chapter 7 "Health Support in the Palm of Your Hand: The Role of Technology in Achieving Health Goals" reviews how Smartphone apps and social network sites are being used by individuals who want to take care of their health, finding suggestions for the individuals who are using digital technologies in order to improve their well-being. It also shows how specific social marketing campaigns can be designed to influence healthcare behavior for particular individuals, including health promotion and interventions to help individuals achieve personal goals and improve the quality of their life.

In Chapter 8 "Universal Health Coverage and Environmental Health: An Investigation in Decreasing Communicable and Chronic Disease by Including Environmental Health in UHC," the authors demonstrate how by implementing country-specific universal healthcare (UHC) approaches, focusing on sufficient government spending on healthcare (including training healthcare professionals) and engaging public-private partnerships to successfully target environmental health at the community level, universal healthcare can be achieved.

Ubaldo Comite
Department of Business and Law
University "Giustino Fortunato"
Benevento, Italy

Chapter 1

Low-Cost Health/Medical Tourism of Italians

Tullio Romita and Antonella Perri

Additional information is available at the end of the chapter

http://dx.doi.org/10.5772/intechopen.69954

Abstract

In recent years, becoming a form of spatial mobility of people is mainly called "medical tourism or health tourism". In Italy the adoption of the expression "turismo sanitario" is often used as an international expression synonymous with "medical tourism or health tourism": this situation raises a number of conceptual problems. In fact, the Italian public health service is one of the most developed in the world and is distinguished by many nations to the fact to offer its citizens free of charge and many health care services. In this situation, the Italian citizen in need of medical care is not convenient to travel to other places and is not obliged to do so. In fact, the Italian citizen tends to move for medical and health care that the Italian public health service does not deliver at no charge: such as dental care, we will deal with this case illustrating some examples of dental tourism low cost of the Italians. However, from our point of view, tourism period may be coupled to the trips to the health or well-being only in cases where the journey is "voluntary." All this will be discussed in this paper.

Keywords: turismo sanitario, health care and low cost, health and holiday

1. Introduction

Expressions like medical tourism or health tourism are very widespread nowadays and for the past 10 years are used to indicate the geographical (territorial) mobility of people moving around the world looking at this way of meeting together the motivations and needs that deal with health and well-being, with needs related recreation, knowledge, and holidays. This kind of mobility has grown more and more over time due to the (considerable) opportunity of visibility by World Wide Web about global health opportunities. In fact, due to World Wide Web, people have the possibility to communicate in real time and the ability to move faster and faster and economically in space, especially through low-cost air transport.

In the contest of health and wellness, there is a real competition between touristic destinations that are increasing their product offerings in order to gain significant shares of this type of tourism market.

However, within the analysis and study of the phenomenon, the first difficulties refer to the theoretical and conceptual problems it generates, especially in the Italian case, the use of the term "health tourism." In this work, we will analyze this particular issue and the low-cost medical tourism of Italians.[1]

2. For a definition of "health/medical tourism"

The term "health/medical tourism" has its origin in those countries where coverage of the cost of medical care is borne by the public or where there is no public health services guaranteed by the state.

This situation is found in several of the Western world rich countries, such as many of the major English-speaking countries (the United States of America), where, in fact, and for a very long time, you can observe a great mobility of people who need medical care and that move within their own country, or even abroad, to the medical service research that, at least of equal quality, offers a more advantageous cost.[2]

However, in countries like Italy where, as always, there is a national health service, that is, where the state offers its citizens the opportunity to care for free or at low cost, and where all the different types of medical services are, or should be, guaranteed locally or, in any case, in the vicinity of the closest spatial urban centers, the health tourism expression has never been, and still it is not today, similarly applicable, on the contrary, said in these terms, it seems inappropriate, that is, because the main reason for medical mobility is determined or because the severity of the person's health situation is such that to resolve it, he must move toward national public specialized centers of medical excellence or because the place where he lives the public health presents evident criticality in the quality of medical services.

Obviously, the reference just mentioned on the Italian situation does not apply to all citizens, in the sense that existing excellent medical services are provided in private health facilities, people who can afford it, that is, those with greater economic capacity, they may decide to opt for this type of medical facilities and not for those public ones.

[1]Paragraphs "Introduction", "For a definition of health/medical tourism" and "Conclusions" are by Tullio Romita; Paragraphs "The so-called 'health tourism' market" and "Low-cost medical tourism of Italians" are by Antonella Perri.
[2]It is also fair to add that mobility is not only directed to having a quality medical service at or higher, but also to search for the so-called "second opinion" as a confirmation of a diagnosis or treatment.

It is favorable to point out that in Europe we have tried to regulate the sector of health services with specific European directive of 2011,[3]establishing the rules for cross-border healthcare, under which European citizens are now allowed to cure themselves freely even in countries other than their own.

In any case, what our opinion appears at this point is necessary that it is to reflect on at least two issues. The first one is whether expressions indicating the so-called "medical tourism" indicate the same phenomenon, even if with different shades, at the international level; the second one is if the mobility of people determined to respond to medical and health needs is in fact appropriate to pair the word "tourism."

Regarding the first question, there is to say that, in the "literature," this kind of tourism is almost always considered substantially equivalent to those of Anglo-Saxon term of "health travel," "medical tourism," or even "Health & Medical Tourism."[4] In fact, however, this situation seems to represent a simplification not useful to understand the differences.

For example, in the Anglo-Saxon world, we are faced with health services, in many cases, paid services and that's why you go looking for economically viable healthcare solutions; this situation assumes the possibility of physical movement, and in these cases, for the same quality of medical service, the choice of where to go can also depend on the attractiveness of the tourist places and/or of the availability of tourist services and leisure. In the Italian case, however, even if a national health service exists, the prevailing gratuity brings the citizen to move to different places than those in which he lives only in the case of particular services or nonexistent or poors at the local level.

In short, from a substantive point of view, the Italian expression "turismo sanitario" does not have the meaning exactly similar to those attributed to the expressions used in the international arena such as "health travel" or "medical tourism." Therefore, in our opinion not even conventionally, in the case of the Italian medical tourism, it appears appropriate to use dogmatically such an expression to propose a comparison with other international experiences, particularly with Anglo-Saxon ones, where, unlike the Italian system, the health services are of private nature, and for that, they are a substantial economic burden to the citizen.

The second issue on which we have set ourselves to reflect on it is whether it is in fact appropriate to use the term "tourism" to indicate the physical mobility of people toward health services, which is currently widespread.

Indeed, technically the use of the term "health tourism" depends by the definition of tourism generally adopted, developed, and proposed by the UNWTO,[5] according to which[6]: "Tourism is a social, cultural, and economic phenomenon, which entails the movement of people to

[3] For a discussion about the cross-border healthcare scheme, see Ref. [1].

[4] In this regard compares, for example, Refs. [2–4].

[5] The UNWTO acronym stands for "United Nations World Tourism Organization"; the corresponding Italian acronym is OMT (Organizzazione Mondiale del Turismo).

[6] The tourism definitions provided by the UNWTO are so many, since tourism is a social phenomenon that continually changes its character, the definitions have gradually over time adapted to ongoing social changes. The definition given refers back to 2014 and it is within the "Glossary of tourism terms" UNWTO [5].

countries or places outside their usual environment for personal or business/professional purposes. These people are called visitors (which may be either tourists or excursionists; residents or nonresidents) and tourism has to do with their activities, some of which involve tourism expenditure." In this regard, it is worth to highlight that the definition of tourism over time has greatly expanded its conceptual meaning, and today, there is a tendency, in fact, to consider tourists even those who move for instrumental purposes (for example, for work reasons), and this leads to a census as a tourist movement, practically all types of travelers regardless the motivation that determines the journey.

In other words, to be tourism, to be able to label a particular territorial mobility of people as a tourist, it would be enough for the presence of a condition: the journey to a destination other than the one where you normally live. While visitors/hikers, even if today conceptually considered tourists, they remain statistically and economically very difficult to evaluate due to the absence of at least one night in an accommodation facility.

Anyway, the definition of tourism provided by the UNWTO and with it, a large capacity to consider substantially as tourism, as we have said before, almost all streams of people who move to places other than their own for us is clearly very difficult to recognize as valid the "health tourism" expression; we see a paradoxical situation in part, in the sense that it seems almost an oxymoron. Here, we try to explain what we mean.

Indeed, contemporary society no longer offers the certainties of modernity and even try to frame the conceptual and theoretical point of view of tourism phenomenon, precisely because social phenomenon of globalized mass and in continuous expansion, it becomes an increasingly difficult operation and contains full of obstacles. However, we think to have some certainties.

In a study of sociology on tourism very well-known internationally and still widely used today, Cohen [6] identified and defined the tourism role based on some dimensions. In other words, according to this scholar, any traveler could call himself a tourist in the presence of the following dimensions: (1) the stay of tourists should be temporary (for this reason they are different from other types of travelers as they have a residence that makes them traceable); (2) the tourist makes a round trip (this distinguishes it from the travelers who move to other places, such as immigrants, permanently); (3) the visitor makes a journey that is not completed in the same day (what differentiates it from hikers travelers); (4) the tourist traveling along pathways that, however, do not occur frequently; (5) tourists in traveling do not pursue instrumental goals (what distinguishes it from business travelers, for example, businessmen, missionaries, politicians, etc.); (6) the tourist is a person who decides to embark on the journey in a totally voluntary way (what distinguishes him from all the travelers who become obliged, for example: victims of political persecution, political prisoners, the prisoners, the sick, etc.) [7].

Cohen's work, although of extremely useful and epistemological interest, we have no difficulty in admitting that by virtue of the important changes that have affected the tourism phenomenon in time, it is no longer present and, moreover, "… It is limited in the real tourist experience. A series of figures traveler would remain outside in which the tourism component has ample space. Consider, for example, hikers, those who decide to spend a day on a farm or under an umbrella at the beach, or even the congressman who takes the opportunity to learn about a new location, it is these situations which are now generally considered to be a constituent part of tourist flows." [7].

Even taking into account the above, by comparing the contents of Cohen's tourism dimensions and the definition of tourism role by UNWTO and adopting a more conceptual flexibility; however, it seems to emerge a broad convergence about who the tourist is and what tourism is. So given things, the aspect that even the definition of tourism UNWTO does not capture is "the voluntary nature of the trip."

This, in our view, remains central to really understand what tourism is distinguishing it from what tourism is not and who tourist is from who is not even when the journey that is accomplished is not voluntary? Can trips really be included in tourist flows that they are required to do?

Using the definition UNWTO, the answer would be, probably, yes! While in the past, the entire mobility made with mostly recreational purposes and entertainment was considered tourism; today, there is a tendency to see the presence of tourist aspects in all types of mobility, and for that, we can conclude on the basis of over-simplifying phrases such as that included in the definition given above by the UNWTO tourism: Tourism is a social, cultural, and economic phenomenon, which entails the movement of people to countries or places outside their usual environment for personal or business/professional purposes.

Indeed, however, can we really think that a person who is working as a sales representative and that every day, he travels for hundreds of kilometers by car, traveling from city to city, even sleeping and eating at several hotels and restaurants, can be counted as tourist mobility? Or that the person who moves from his home to go to work for 6 months a year in another place and in doing so also sleeps and eats in various hotels and restaurants, can it be counted as a tourist mobility? Or also, and more simply, can it be considered a tourist the parent obligated to visit a university student son in need of help, and in doing so, he spent a short time in a holiday complex located in a distant city? From our point of view, the answer to these questions is probably not! The voluntary nature of the trip remains an essential element of tourism; otherwise, we are talking about something else and not of tourism.[7]

Also, since it does not solve the problem of voluntariness of the trip, we think that the simplification of Henderson [8] is not very useful and that it has encouraged the definition of the various areas of "health tourism" dividing the search for cures into four categories: (1) the area of disease conditions (all forms of surgical interventional, diagnostic investigations, etc.); (2) the wellness area that can encompass the so-called alternative medicines as well as spa treatments and fitness; (3) the area of esthetic enhancement through plastic and cosmetic surgery; (4) the breeding area for fertility treatments and assisted reproduction.

---

[7]An interesting aspect that should be investigated, is that inherent to the paradox mentioned by Lunt et al. [9] that one side he talks about the voluntary nature of the trip, but on the other, highlights the preference of patients to be treated close to home. This in our view would justify an attitude obvious and immediate that equal of quality medical, patients, even for economic reasons, tend to choose the closest specific center.

Ultimately, based on the principle of voluntariness of the journey becomes really difficult to see if and when it is possible in the Italian case, the use of the term "health tourism," an expression, in our opinion, that to represent the phenomenon is more just separate into two further expressions: "medical trip" and "wellness tourism":

- With the "medical trip" expression, we could indicate all those travel experiences that individuals make because in any case obliged, the motivation of the travel to seek health care controls and/or medical treatment that they are necessary to the control or to the resolution of a disease, though the related medical and health care services are available at the place where he usually lives;
- With the "wellness tourism" expression, we could, however, indicate all volunteer's trips that people make for not essential medical services but for the care of the psycho-physical wellness of their appearance. Among other things, it is worth noting that in the Italian case, the public national health service does not recognize the costs of nearly all of these treatments, which are therefore the sole responsibility of the citizen, and even if the choice of the medical structure in which "you receive care" is important, it is important too, the identification of the place where to go that sometimes convinces in particular the offer of "tourist" services associated, in other words to mix business and pleasure.

In the first case, that one of "medical trip," we find ourselves faced with a necessary journey, where the only motivation is the need for appropriate treatment, maybe only available in certain cities and medical facilities. Although for these purposes, you may need to go in very desirable locations, or use the magnificent tourist services, it is difficult to think that this kind of travel experience is actually a tourism experience. In the second case, that one of "wellness tourism," are faced with travel volunteers, either because not necessary from a medical point of view or because the health services are generally widespread or available in the places where you live, in any event, services not absolutely necessary for the very survival of the person. Moreover, in the case of "medical trip," the challenge to attract the attention of the person as a "traveler" is not based on the tourist attractiveness of the destination, but on the presence of medical facilities and onto high quality or unique health services (in this case, the choice of where and how to stay will depend more easily by logistical and/or economic parameters). While in the case of "wellness tourism," not only the choice is based on availability and quality of services and healthcare type structures, but also on the attractiveness of the tourist destination, on the different and qualified availability of tourism services, and reachability of the destination (the most obvious case is that of dental care, where in the last decade has developed an international challenge, with dozens of different offer packages that include in addition to medical care, travel, accommodation, excursions in the area, and an increasingly wide range of additional services for leisure).

In conclusion, we recognize as not useful and misleading using the term "health tourism," at least in the Italian case. The reasoning led us first of all to separate the expression into two parts to start to understand more fully the phenomenon: we think we can establish that the "medical trip" is obligated by its nature, and therefore, it is not considered as tourism, as is the related traveler cannot be considered a tourist but, a "person in need of medical care"; the "wellness tourism" is, however, more properly defined as "health tourism," because the more easily the nature of the trip is voluntary and the ability to care about their psycho-physical wellness reconciles with the tourist experience that assumes knowledge of the places where you are traveling and the development of relations and knowledge relations with host populations.[8]

3. The so-called "health tourism" market

Evaluate the value of world market of so-called "health tourism" is not easy for two reasons.

The first one is a question of conceptual character. As we wrote before, to establish with reasonable accuracy what actually "health tourism" is, it is possible only when you come to a shared definition of the meaning. However, for the purposes of this paper, we assume that health tourism like all mobility that is determined by motives that concern as well as medical care dedicated to the more general welfare of the people. The second reason is the scarcity of systematic studies of this type of mobility, for which you will use what we currently have.

Bearing in mind the considerations just made, we say that already about 10 years ago, the American company Deloitte Research [10] predicted a rosy future for the US health tourism, which it imagined would touch the six million citizens compared to about eight hundred thousand in 2007, for a global turnover estimated at several billion dollars annually.

The same Deloitte [11], in a later study calculated "… that every year seven million people in the world travel because of health reasons, already generating a turnover of 100 billion dollars, which will become 150 in 2018" [12]. In addition, according to another study dated 2016, "… the revenue generated from medical tourism already amounted to 12 billion euro in Europe … Italy has a market share of 2 billion, which could reach 4, by implementing the "provision of health and tourism services offered to foreigners."[9]

The so-called health tourism is today a social and economic phenomenon of great importance in fact recently, and for the first time in one of the most important fairs of world tourism, which was the FITUR 2015, a specific space it has been reserved right to health tourism.

However, the Italian Association for Medical Tourism Development (IAMT) has published on its website [13], a brief illustration of the background of health tourism. In particular, the variables that determine the majority of the customer mobility flows are the quality of the delivered treatments; better access to health services; the absence of waiting lists; the ability to bind to a health need for the satisfaction of a tourist needs; travel opportunities; the cost of treatment, which is a significant variable for a given segment of the market; the confidentiality, especially for esthetic interventions. In addition, with regard to the health tourism numbers, it notes that about 15 million tourists patients in 2017 will decide to resort to medical treatment abroad, and that the major destinations of health tourism for many tourists are Costa Rica, India, Israel, Malaysia, Mexico, Singapore, South Korea, Taiwan, Thainlandia, Turkey, and United States of America.

[8]In this paper, our intention is to consider the tourist as a person with an emphasis on the human and the emotional aspect. Not included in the health consumer commodification process, but as a person who seeks a better state of health.
[9]Forum on the Internationalization of the Italian Health 2016, Rome; Report Observatory Private Consumption in Health (OCPS), SDA Bocconi, Milan.

There are more than 200,000 Italians who are traveling because of sanitary issues. At least, a quarter of this, 200,000 Italians ask for medical care dentistry. Most treatments in specialized health tourism dental are in Eastern European countries, Croatia, Hungary, and Romania (with Albania that's growing up). For the Italians, it is easy to get there in these countries, especially if they live near the airport. It is quite clear that these are countries where the cost of dental care is much lower than in Italy. Often the dentists (in these countries) have even studied abroad. The promotion of health treatment is very aggressive and aims almost exclusively on the Web support; in addition, all medical treatments are combined, with the basic tourist services like accommodation, food, shuttle service, etc. and excursions in the area who takes care to these tourists who speak Italian.

Precisely of this type of health tourism, we will deal in the next section.

4. Low-cost medical tourism of Italians

In this section, we will deal with the case of the health travels of Italians to foreign destinations where there are specialized institutions in dental care.

Thousands of Italians are contacting low-cost dental clinics in countries belonging mainly to Eastern Europe, and as we have mentioned before, it is a growing phenomenon.

Countries such as Croatia, Bulgaria, Romania, Slovenia, Poland, and Albania are in the last years the European leaders in dental health tourism market.

In recent years, we are seeing a proliferation of so-called low-cost dental centers, or commercial chains, mostly franchised, offer dental services at low prices.

Several clinics offer "all inclusive packages" at very low prices. In the "all inclusive," beyond the costs directly attributable to the dental expenses in the strict sense, in many cases, the costs of travel, the stay in the place where the clinic and excursions in the area is located are included.

The very low cost relative to the "all inclusive package," is due, according to what these clinics confirm, to the fact that "everything costs less" than the other countries of Western Europe: the rental of commercial premises, the average salary of a dentist, the cost of electricity, water, heating, expenses for advertising, administrative costs, taxes [14]. Indeed, the Italian president of the National Council of dentists, Dr. Giuseppe Renzo, in a 2015 interview said that "Italians look for alternative health services to cope with the crisis period" and because of the high prices of dental care in Italy according to Istat "over 8 million citizens would prefer not to heal mouth and teeth." In fact, in an article in the Italian newspaper "Il fatto quotidiano" in talking about low-cost dental tourism is reported an interview with an Apulian lady who alleged that she was aware of the possible risks to go to Albania to dental care, but the Italian prices would not have permitted to care of her teeth; moreover, it would have taken little time to arrive in Albania, and that she was very satisfied with the reception saying "they treat me like a queen, they cuddle me, they offer me the stay and make me visit the castles" [15]. Furthermore, Dr. Renzo stated that "dentistry in Italy is based in large part on a private network of professional firms whose basic costs are on average four times higher than those faced by professionals from other countries. The tax is 22% compared to 4; VAT cannot be deducted; the costs for collaborators are a weight on the cost, but their presence is essential to ensure safety and hygiene" [16]. On the other hand, the Italian dentists assign to the low cost of dental services low quality [17], mainly with respect to sanitary regulations, the respect of clinicians time, and the necessity of subsequent checks [18].

The dental tourism in recent years has made its history to Albania. There are several clinics on the Albanian territory, as many are also, the individual dental practices. Among the different realities encountered in our research, we wanted to analyze the case of "Dentists in Albania–Viaggiare e sorridere" [19].

In their Web page, they immediately show the fact that in Albania many of them speak, even correctly, the Italian (75% of the population) putting the possible Italian customer at ease and reassuring him, as well, also, they reassure on professionalism and quality of materials used (that they define high), they perform the relevant certifications and that they offer 5 years Warranty [20].

Albanian dentists reassure the potential customers on the qualitative aspect of their services, explain why their prices are so low compared to Italian dentists, attributing the reason to lower taxes, saying that in Albania tax pressure affects 10% while in Italy 55%, and the lower labor costs are due to a lower cost of living. In their opinion, it would lead to savings for the Italian patient tourists by 60% compared to what they could spend in Italy.

Another element that it should entice potential Italian customers to turn to them is the so-called word of mouth. In fact, on the website, dozens of testimonials were published that highlight the quality of services offered, the main motivation of the trip, that is, the economic issue and the tourist aspect. A witness, in fact, declares: "I hope nobody feels offended, I want just to tell my experience: in Italy, our doctors charge 4 times the cost of performances more than the Albanians, often abusing of the good faith of our patients and of our lack of information with the result of a medical service of the third world! This is what happened to me in Italy. That's why I want everyone to know about my experience with Viaggiare e sorridere. In Albania, for three certified dental implants made in Europe and the extraction of teeth 3, I spent EUR 1,400.00, and I was operated by a skilled doctor, who teaches Dental Implantology at the University of Tirana and by her husband too. The intervention lasted only 55 minutes as opposed to Italy, in fact the Italian dentists to justify the excessive price make you go several times ending up losing even 3 months. I saw people from all social backgrounds enter in this clinic equipped with the best three-dimensional machinery and hygiene at par with the best clinics in the world, I saw people, which they hugged each to other and then they decided to exchange they phone numbers, people pleased to have found a smile without signing a mortgage. A unique professionalism, many money saved and the stay is free, as also the taxi for and by Tirana to airport on arrival and departure and outings to discover the beauty of their land with the company of reception staff who speak Italian. A real holiday of well-being, which is why I thank and advise everyone the clinic Viaggiare e sorridere" [21]. Among other things, each patient/tourist who has left his testimony has left their contact information in case any potential customer wants to know more.

In Albania, low prices are not the only element to attract customers' attention, there are other elements as: a detailed range of interventions and services offered, the curriculum of some dentists and professionals who are part of the medical staff and not, the reviews (all positive) of their patients/tourists; "Dentists in Albania" also uses the "card" of the holiday, offering, among other things, a free stay for two people, and both the transfer to the hotel and the reception service: at the airport, there will be an attendant who will speak properly in Italian and that he will welcome them, he will be available to patients-tourists from 9 AM to 21 PM to resolve any problems on the stay or even to play the role of tour guide of the city. In addition, the reception agent will be available 24–24h contacting him by telephone. Even before the trip, they offer their availability to clients in the organization of the trip, advising how to reach Tirana "stress-free and save a lot of money." The tourist aspect is repeatedly quoted on the website where, among other things, you can read "beyond to low-cost professional dental care, you will have the opportunity to take a holiday in a wonderful city like Tirana, all without spending just a euro for the stay and benefiting of all the services that you want."

It is some years now, that some of these dental clinics have opened offices in Italy where they exclusively, do free visits with the purpose of provide quotes. Among them, there is the case "Dentists Croatia low-cost," which opened an office in Verona for "a free estimate, to explain the treatments, prices, to answer all your questions freely, and to give you all the information related to your stay in Croatia."

For free, no-obligation appointments call us at our number "...Cell...Email..." [22]. Also in this case, the bus trip, starting from some cities reported on the website, is free. It is to be noted that accommodation is free sometimes subjected to the cost of the performance that a patient goes to support it and, in any case, the patient's accommodation does not happen in a hotel but in an apartment. In particular, the dental office specifies: "During your dental care, we offer a FREE comfortable apartment in the center of RIJEKA/RIVER Croatia near the sea with five beds. The apartment is free if you spend at least € 1000/1500 in dental care" [23].

Actually, in this case, by some researches carried out on the Web, it is not a dental clinic, but it concerns a real travel agency that manages the health travels. Indeed, by analyzing other websites offering low-cost dental care in Croatia, we realized that another website had the same addresses of "Dentists Croatia low-cost," and it is the following website www.viaggideldente.info [24]. The latter, it is known as the "Tour operator of dental savings," offering free travels by bus from some cities in northern Italy, low-cost dental care "in the best dental practice in Croatia" [25] and the opportunity to book your stay at favorable prices in the apartment.

However, the proliferation of dental clinics and dental low-cost studies in recent years has become an increasingly important phenomenon, and, therefore, the online offering of low-cost dental tourism is really impressive. Even in Italy dental centers specialized low cost are springing to try to attract these patients/tourists who want to be cured at a lower price. Although, now, as we have seen, competition in the European scenario, in terms of cost and quality, it really is ever more.

5. Conclusion

In our discussion of the issue, we refer to the patient/tourist in terms of an exaltation of humanity. We refer to the person and his emotional sphere, which led him to travel to search for a better state of health [26]. Rests in the economic and marketing logic and activates processes for which he becomes a consumer, but he remains a person driven by doubts, fragility, and hope to the pursuit of happiness.

The medical treatment related to dental care is among the categories of health (medical) tourism, which refers to disease conditions and to ones of the esthetic improvement.

The research shows that the main reasons why Italians do dental care abroad are due to saving time and money. As well as because distance, communication, and knowledge of the language are not a real problem. Finally, using in a wise way the Web, there is no needs either of large economic investments to create promotion nor advertisements [27].

Italy is not among the top destinations for foreign health tourism, even if relying on a health care system, it is between the most efficient in the world. Italy was always been one of the most important tourist destinations in the world. Because of this, it is possible to arrange strategies that allow Italy to grow up the market related to the health tourism.

Acknowledgements

The authors would like to thank Dr. Lucia Groe. This research was supported by her who provided expertise and comments that greatly improved the manuscript.

Author details

Tullio Romita* and Antonella Perri

*Address all correspondence to: tullio.romita@unical.it

Università della Calabria, Rende, CS, Italy

References

[1] The European Directive 2011/24 of 9 March 2011

[2] Schael T, Rinaldi P. Globalizzazione in sanità. Il paziente diventa turista. VoiceCom news. 2010:37-46. marzo

[3] Schael T, Ballotta P. Strategie di attrazione per il turismo sanitario in Italia, XVII Convegno Nazionale. Rome: AIES; 2012

[4] Rossi A. Strategie per il turismo sanitario. Le componenti di una strategia di internazionalizzazione dei servizi sanitari. Health & Medicine, Marzo. 2014

[5] UNWTO. Glossary of tourism terms, Last update: February 2014. Available from: http://www2.unwto.org/en [22-02-2017]

[6] Cohen E. Who is a Tourist? A conceptual clarification. The Sociological Review. 1974;**22**(4):527-554

[7] Romita T. Argomenti di sociologia del turismo, Working Paper n.78. Università della Calabria; Messina; 2010. pp. 9-10

[8] Henderson JC. Healthcare tourism in Southeast Asia. Tourism Review International. 2004(7):111-122

[9] Lunt N, Horsfall D, Hanefeld J. Handbook on Medical Tourism and Patient Mobility. Elgar; UK; 2015

[10] Deloitte. Medical Tourism: Consumers in Search of Value. Deloitte Center for Health Solutions; New York; 2008 (See www.deloitte.com/centerforhealthsolutions)

[11] Deloitte. 2014 Global Health Care Outlook. Shared Challenges, Shared Opportunities. New York; 2014. pp. 1-24 (Web)

[12] http://www.lastampa.it/2016/09/21/italia/cronache/turismo-sanitario-anche-litalia-una-eccellenza-C8OG1I0WQf3OoFT7JCjtyH/pagina.html. Available from: [22-02-2017]

[13] http://www.iamt.it/?page_id=37

[14] http://turismodentale.al/Turismo-Dentale/Perche-prezzi-piu-bassi/perche-prezzi-piu-bassi.html

[15] http://www.ilfattoquotidiano.it/2017/01/15/albania-patria-del-turismo-dentale-low-cost-le-protesi-con-la-vacanza-intorno-odontoiatri-italiani-concorrenza-al-ribasso/3212554/

[16] http://www.ilgiornale.it/news/sirena-delle-cure-low-cost-farebbe-bis-soltanto-paziente-su-1085991.html

[17] http://www.odontotecnici.net/news/2009/097articolo2009.htm

[18] http://www.dentistiassociati.org/impianti-dentali/turismo-dentale-i-dentisti-in-croazia-sono-unopportunita-o-un-rischio/

[19] http://www.dentistiinalbania.com/

[20] http://www.dentistiinalbania.com/garanzia-sicurezza-igiene-orale/

[21] http://www.dentistiinalbania.com/testimonianze-dentisti-dentista-estero-croazia-ungheria-romania/

[22] http://dentistacroazia.eu/it/il-nostro-ufficio-a-rimini-per-preventivi-gratis.html

[23] http://dentistacroazia.eu/it/appartamento-in-croazia-gratis.html

[24] www.viaggideldente.info

[25] https://www.viaggideldente.info/appartamento-a-fiume-rijeka.html

[26] Fondazione ISTUD. Dalla sanità tradizionale a percorsi di nuova economia: la sanità low cost: rapporto di ricerca, XI edizione del "Programma scienziati in azienda", Stresa; 2010

[27] Garcìa-Altès A. The development of heath tourism services, Annals of Tourism Research. 2005;**32**(Jan):262-266

Chapter 2

The Future Population Health of the Industrialized Countries

Pietro Iaquinta

Additional information is available at the end of the chapter

http://dx.doi.org/10.5772/67819

Abstract

The more developed countries are experiencing an inexorable decline with respect to population. Aging is reaching intolerable levels in the economy, both from the active (available workers) and the passive (e.g. health costs, pensions) point of view, redesigning a worrying scenario for the near future. On the other hand, fertility in many countries, and particularly in Italy, reaches such low levels that the prospects of a recovery, in terms of quantity, now seem impractical, unless of socio-demographic upheavals rather unlikely. In this context, most likely, from the point of view of demographic and social, he is starting a new era in which the main actors on the global stage will certainly be different from those in the field today, with completely obscure scenarios and still in the making. Surely, however, this situation has generated fears and concerns about the future of the population, especially for some signals that in the course of 2015 were recorded in Italy, such as the surge in mortality, especially with regard to older ages, where some observers have linked this phenomenon to a reduction in public spending in the health sector, a situation that would have penalized, certainly, the older age groups. On closer analysis, however, we realize that, precisely due to aging of the population of elderly, quotas have gradually increased, causing a swollen available to die, with the same probability of death.

Keywords: population, health, labor market, fertility, development

1. Introduction

The more developed countries are experiencing an inexorable decline with respect to the population. Aging is reaching intolerable levels in the economy, both from the active (available workers) and the passive (e.g. health costs, pensions) point of view, redesigning a worrying scenario for the near future.

On the other hand, fertility in many countries, and particularly in Italy, reaches such low levels that the prospects of a recovery, in terms of quantity, now seem impractical, unless of socio-demographic upheavals rather unlikely.

In this context, most likely, from the point of view of demographic and social, he is starting a new era in which the main actors on the global stage will certainly be different from those in the field today, with completely obscure scenarios and still in the making.

Surely, however, this situation has generated fears and concerns about the future of the population, especially for some signals that in the course of 2015 were recorded in Italy, such as the surge in mortality, especially with regard to older ages, where some observers have linked this phenomenon to a reduction in public spending in the health sector, a situation that would have penalized, certainly, the older age groups. On closer analysis, however, we realize that, precisely due to aging of the population of elderly, quotas have gradually increased, causing a swollen available to die, with the same probability of death.

We are at the dawn of a new world, and the population of the planet will be substantially transformed over the next 30–40 years, according to the latest update made by the World Bank (World Population Prospects: The 2015 Revision. New York: United Nations). The world population has reached 7 billion people in 2015 and will rise to 9 billion around 2050, an increase due mainly to developing countries.

But the most significant fact is that few countries will contribute to more than half the increase worldwide, especially this will be due to the contribution of India, Pakistan, Nigeria, Ethiopia, the United States, Congo, Tanzania, China, and Bangladesh.

The World Bank, which had already produced in the 1980s of the projections that had left the whole world into turmoil, when it predicted that the world population would reach 20 billion people already in 2020, has, as a precautionary measure, developed based on the assumption that projections fertility decline through woman from the current global level of 2.5 children to 2.1, from now until 2050. Population of the 49 least developed countries is growing still faster than the rest of the world, at a pace of 2–3% a year, as published by the Population Division.

While it is expected that the population of developing countries as a whole will increase from 6 billion today to 7.9 billion in 2050, the population of more developed regions will not change much, passing from 1.23 to 1.28 billion.

The latter would have had to decrease to 1.15 billion were it not for the projected net rate of migration from developing countries to developed countries, which provides for the annual shift of about 2–2.5 million people over the next 30–40 years.

Also, according to the projections of the World Bank, the scenario is even more disheartening for Europe, as a whole, in fact, to the middle of the twenty-first century the population of the old continent not even reach 8% of the world's population and, even more worrying, this will be characterized by a high seniority, against the rest of the world, however, will feature a very young population

2. Some consideration about Italian population

The demographic structure of population of all developed countries, and especially that of Italy, has been shaped, as is stated in any book of demographic analysis, by the effect of great transformations that have powered the path of evolution in the twentieth century in general and since the end of the Second World War in particular.

Great structural movements that have characterized the evolution of the Italian population in the long term were initially that of the *demographic transition*, then the era of *baby boom* and finally the *low-low fertility*.

The demographic transition,[1] in fact, marks the passage of a population from an archaic development model, characterized essentially by high levels of fertility and mortality, a structure of particularly young age and a hierarchical disorder between parents and children [1][2] (the latter dying before the former in large numbers) to a model of modern development, with values 10 of birth rates and death rates particularly low (and stable), a structure of much older age, and with the restoration of a more normal hierarchical order in the chronology of deaths between children and parents.

In the completion of the demographic transition process, the values of the quotients of natality and mortality pass from rather high levels, even around 40–60% to much lower values which, at the end of the process, can reach values even around 7–8% (**Figure 1** and **Table 1**, as regards Italy). This underlines a transformation of the vivacity of the natural movements: before the transition, the situation is characterized by many births and many premature deaths (with a large number of children deaths); after the transition, the situation is characterized by fewer births but with the lengthening of life span [2] due to the collapse of mortality in younger ages (known as infant mortality).

In case of the birth rate, the reduction process is uniquely determined by the inexorable reduction in births and by an important increase in procreation age of the mother (but also of

---

[1]Scheme generalized by the trend of birth rates and death rates in the period of the demographic transition.

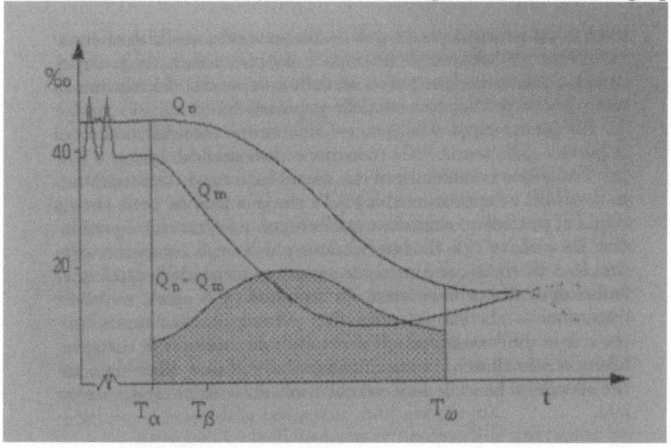

[2]Livi Bacci, which emphasizes how this problem was actually at the base of the high birth rates. In essence, the couples (or families) produced more children in order to guarantee in the long term the survival of at least some of them, given the high level of mortality during childhood.

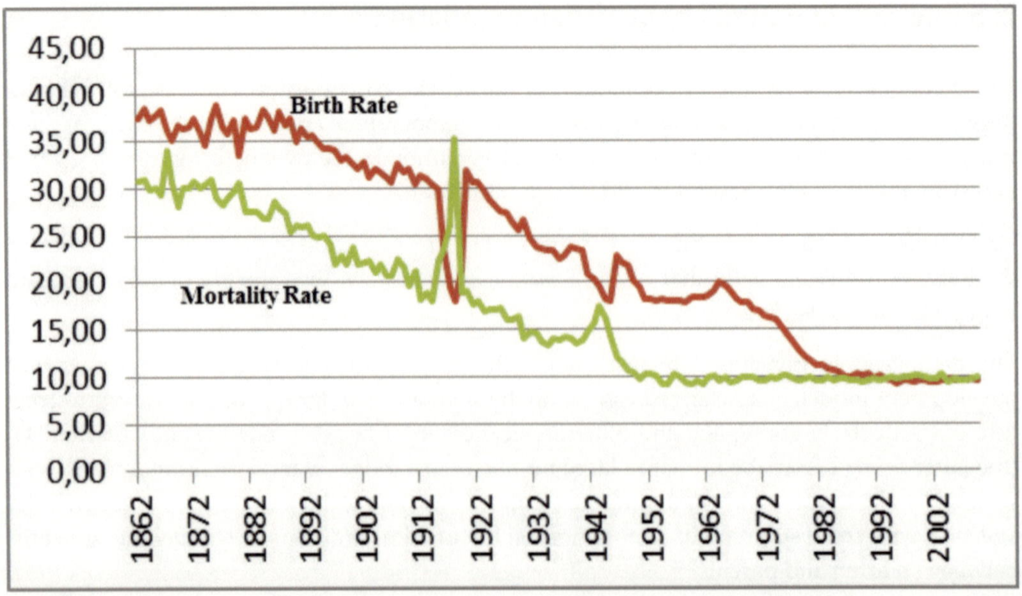

Figure 1. Evolution of natality and mortality quotients in Italy, 1862–2015.[6] Source: our elaboration on ISTAT's data. [6]Figure loosely based on and adapted from Iaquinta [7].

the father) [3–5][3] [4] especially the "primiparous mother," whereas in case of the reduction path of mortality ratios and therefore mortality in general, there are many factors involved in its determination, because mortality is distributed in all age groups with a gradually increasing incidence.

The baby boom, however, which takes place temporarily at least in Italy around the end of the demographic transition process, is a typically Italian phenomenon. In this phenomenon, because of the contraction due to the traumatic effects of the Second World War, strong economic expansion of the 1960s is associated with a sharp increase in births such as to reach the point to return to pre-conflict levels, in the presence, however, of a period in which the mortality (especially infant mortality) lowering effect keeps alive a large number of births well beyond that found previously [2].

[3]These concepts have already been widely anticipated and explored in numerous scientific papers, including, in particular, we point out P. Iaquinta—T. Traversa, Evoluzione della fecondità nelle società post-transizionali, the paper presented at the Giornate di Studio della Popolazione, Milano 20-22 febbraio 2001; P. Iaquinta, *La fecondità in Italia. Integrazione ed omogeneizzazione dei dati con modellistica ARIMA*, in G. Da Molin, Prospettive di ricerca, Collana "Saggi e Ricerche" del Dipartimento di Scienze storiche e geografiche, n° 34, Bari, 2003; P. Iaquinta, *Some consideration about fertility in Italy. Methodological Problems*, International Area Review, Hankuk University of Foreign Studies, Korea, vol. 6, N°. 2, Fall 2003.
[4]Figure loosely based on and adapted from the text: P. Iaquinta, *Crisi di mortalità: il contributo delle interruzioni volontarie di gravidanza*, in P. B. Helzel – A. J. Katolo, *Autorità e crisi dei poteri*, Cedam, Padova, 2012.

Year	Births	Year	Births	Year	Births
1926	1,094,587	**1956**	873,608	**1986**	555,445
1927	1,093,772	**1957**	878,906	**1987**	551,539
1928	1,072,316	**1958**	870,468	**1988**	569,698
1929	1,037,700	**1959**	901,017	**1989**	560,688
1930	1,092,678	**1960**	910,192	**1990**	569,255
1931	1,026,197	**1961**	929,657	**1991**	562,787
1932	990,995	**1962**	937,257	**1992**	567,841
1933	995,979	**1963**	960,336	**1993**	549,484
1934	992,966	**1964**	1,016,120	**1994**	533,050
1935	996,708	**1965**	990,458	**1995**	525,609
1936	962,686	**1966**	979,940	**1996**	528,103
1937	991,867	**1967**	948,772	**1997**	534,462
1938	1,037,180	**1968**	930,172	**1998**	531,548
1939	1,040,213	**1969**	932,466	**1999**	523,463
1940	1,046,479	**1970**	901,472	**2000**	538,999
1941	937,546	**1971**	906,182	**2001**	528,876
1942	926,063	**1972**	888,203	**2002**	509,340
1943	882,105	**1973**	874,546	**2003**	513,657
1944	814,746	**1974**	868,882	**2004**	546,989
1945	815,678	**1975**	827,852	**2005**	549,110
1946	1,036,098	**1976**	781,638	**2006**	556,427
1947	1,011,490	**1977**	741,103	**2007**	564,365
1948	1,005,851	**1978**	709,043	**2008**	569,366
1949	937,146	**1979**	670,221	**2009**	564,573
1950	908,622	**1980**	640,401	**2010**	561,944
1951	860,998	**1981**	623,103	**2011**	546,607
1952	844,447	**1982**	619,097	**2012**	534,186
1953	839,478	**1983**	601,928	**2013**	514,308
1954	870,689	**1984**	587,871	**2014**	502,596
1955	869,333	**1985**	577,345	**2015**	485,780

Source: ISTAT, Data warehouse, 2017.

Table 1. Live births in Italy, 1926–2015.

This effect made a high portion of births reach the adult age and hence it would be more appropriate to speak of *living boom* rather than *baby boom*; in fact, before the Second World War, about 30% of births did not reach the age of 5, in the 1960–1970s, this proportion already fell to about 3% [6], and in the future, thanks to the contribution of the infamous therapeutic interruption of pregnancy [7], it might fall very easily below 0.3–0.4%, reducing by hundred times the impact of mortality on the survival of the younger generations.

The great economic crisis of the Western world, which started at the beginning of the 1970s, constitutes actually the divide between an old and a new world, in which the powerful and extraordinary parameter of post-bellum development has to come to terms with a new world order.

Perhaps, for the first time, after the feast of progress and indiscriminate growth of the post-Second World War, the Western world is forced to come to terms with a new incumbent danger that hits it: the great oil crisis. This is a crisis, far from being just a purely economic one; in fact, it entails a reconsideration of the entire developed world, calling into question priorities and needs of the entire modern world.

To this situation, dramatic to some extent, countries react with a structural change which also involves the most basic units of social life, such as the family, featuring its new roles, its structure, and especially its composition.

It is at this point that takes shape in Italy the era of *Low-Low Fertility* [8], a time in which the level of fertility of Italian women reaches values which will not be in a position to ensure the replacement of generations (but similar events were experienced in France, Germany, and the Scandinavian countries).

The number of annual births in Italy precipitates from 1,016,000 births in 1964 to around 500,000 since the 1980s, inexorably sealing the fate of the Italian population in terms of both the reproductive capacity and the age structure, which is bound to have a lot of old people beyond any imagination.

Profound behavioral changes in the population, especially those quantitative ones, with respect to the demographic events, have an impact at easily recognizable intervals on the dynamic of labor market entry and exit, respectively, after 20 years in the case of entry and after 60 years in the case of exit.

This simple consideration opens new scenarios of the labor market: if it is true that in the 1960s there were births double those in the 1990s, roughly a quarter of a century later, these births (which, among other things, took place in the living boom era) will present themselves at the entrance of the world of work. Situation will be more regrettable when more or less after 30–35 years from this circumstance, these same generations will approach the exit threshold of the world of work, especially because the next generations born in the era of low-low fertility will not be so large as to ensure the replacement of those in exit.

This will highlight, in a short time, an irreversible condition: the number of people in exit will exceed by far that in entry into the labor market suffocated by the level of unemployment which these first five years of global economic crisis highlighted in a stringent way.

3. Labor market and demography

To evaluate the possible scenario for the next generations, in terms of world of work and employment recovery, a comparison between the generations of people willing to enter the labor market and those willing to exit from it was made to analyze what might happen in the near future as a result of the demographic changes that have characterized the Italian socio-economic life after the Second World War.

To estimate the quantitative effects of the baby boom and low-low fertility on the population, two age groups temporarily willing to turnover were chosen, and a possible future scenario was built projecting the population data.

From the methodological point of view, the age groups relevant to this examination are that of 20–30 years willing to enter the labor market and that of 60–70 years willing to exit from it.

Then, a projection of the Italian population was made with the classic method, using as initial data the population enrolled in the registry office in 2016, the mortality table of 2012, the series of specific quotients of fertility by age of 2011.

The data used were derived from the official source (ISTAT) and were chosen because these were the most currently available in their specific nature, emphasizing that we are making hypothesis on evolutionary scenarios and approximations.

Also available are excellent forecasts built with self-modeling regression and moving average model (ARMA and ARIMA). Even though such models are precise and effective, these results, being available only in an aggregate form compared to the initial data, do not allow us to isolate the various components in order to assess the influence of any politico-social choice that

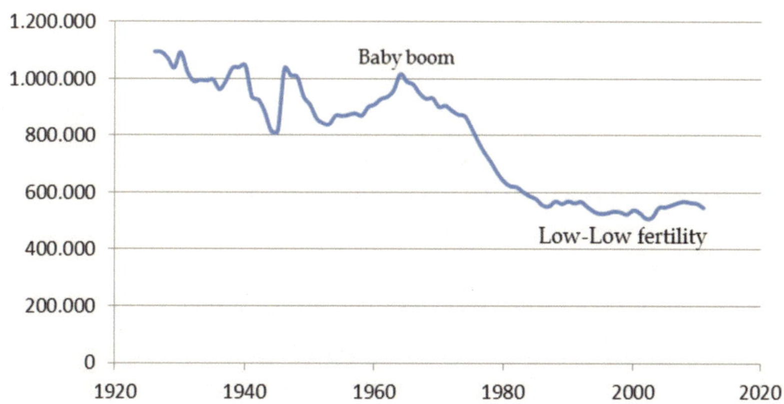

Figure 2. Live births in Italy, 1926–2015. Source: our elaboration on ISTAT's data, warehouse, 2017.

should be taken in the near future. In essence, therefore, the possibility to isolate the components of natality, mortality, and migration in the elaboration of projections allows us to make more probable assumptions about the future of the population itself.

Table 1 and **Figure 2** show the evolution of the number of births between the first quarter of the last century and the present day. **Table 1** highlights the specific trend of the natality level, which affected and still continues to affect the social life in Italy.

Until the Second World War, the birth level was still maintained high in values consistently above the million births per year, with inevitable fluctuations due, in large part, to the approaching of the great crisis that would lead to disastrous conflict.

In any case, the last conflict represented a sort of "threshold value," a kind of divide between the old and the new world, also from the behavioral point of view in relation to the demographic events and to the reproductive process in particular.

In addition, the years after the Great War are also the years in which the reconstruction begins: Italy laboriously starts to develop and this goes at the same rate with great (demographic) achievements such as the sudden collapse of infant mortality.

4. Italian population projection

As mentioned, in order to properly estimate the structure of the Italian population in the coming years and, above all, in order to be able to isolate the components contextually involved in such a determination, it was chosen to make standard projections in an autonomous way so as to govern the individual variables and, eventually, assume alternative hypotheses on the individual components which interact in the formation of the future population.

In order to build the projections, the age structure of the population was derived from the official statistics ISTAT 2017, the latest available data [9]. The table of mortality, used to infer the survival rates [9], aimed to project the population in the next quinquennial age group, was available for 2010; the specific fertility [10] quotients by age were of 2011 (**Tables 2a–c**).

This heterogeneity of reference period must not be misleading in the projection framework, where the choices made are sufficiently aleatory and do not significantly affect the final data.

Rather, it should be clear that we are talking about future hypothesis, estimates, and, therefore, plausible (but certainly not real) values; one argument against it could rather be dictated by the fact that current indicators are largely used in referring to very variable demographic phenomena in order to estimate behaviors in the events of even 40 years ahead.

In any case, before going on, it would be better to underline some methodological limits of this technique, which may affect the results and, therefore, the indicators derived from them.

http://dx.doi.org/10.5772/67819

Age classes	Female 01/01/2016	Px=Lx+s/Lx	Female population projected at the 01-01								
			2021	**2026**	**2031**	**2036**	**2041**	**2046**	**2051**	**2056**	**2061**
0–4	1250,442	0.999474	1143,505	1044,171	980,584	940,876	906,465	858,629	796,235	734,297	684,085
5–9	1385,255	0.999615	1249,785	1142,903	1043,622	980,068	940,381	905,989	858,177	795,817	733,911
10–14	1384,866	0.999399	1384,721	1249,303	1142,463	1043,220	979,690	940,018	905,640	857,847	795,510
15–19	1391,122	0.999078	1384,034	1383,889	1248,553	1141,777	1042,594	979,102	939,454	905,096	857,331
20–24	1472,791	0.999053	1389,839	1382,758	1382,613	1247,401	1140,724	1041,632	978,199	938,587	904,261
25–29	1607,399	0.998796	1471,396	1388,522	1381,448	1381,303	1246,219	1,139,643	1,040,645	977,272	937,698
30–34	1761,403	0.998214	1605,464	1469,624	1386,850	1379,784	1379,640	1,244,719	1,138,271	1,039,392	976,095
35–39	2037,299	0.997132	1758,257	1602,596	1466,999	1384,373	1377,320	1,377,176	1,242,495	1,136,238	1,037,536
40–44	2399,975	0.995115	2031,457	1753,215	1598,000	1462,792	1380,403	1,373,370	1,373,226	1,238,932	1,132,979
45–49	2490,023	0.992087	2388,251	2021,533	1744,650	1590,194	1455,647	1373,660	1,366,661	1,366,518	1,232,880
50–54	2420,239	0.987580	2470,319	2369,353	2005,537	1730,845	1577,611	1444,128	1,362,790	1,355,847	1,355,705
55–59	2110,923	0.981367	2390,181	2439,639	2339,926	1980,629	1709,349	1558,018	1,426,192	1,345,865	1,339,008
60–64	1891,237	0.970783	2071,590	2345,644	2394,181	2296,326	1943,723	1677,498	1,528,987	1,399,618	1,320,787
65–69	1927,499	0.952879	1835,981	2011,064	2277,111	2324,230	2229,235	1886,934	1,628,487	1,484,315	1,358,725
70–74	1533,451	0.916280	1836,673	1749,468	1916,301	2169,812	2214,710	2124,191	1,798,019	1,551,751	1,414,372
75–79	1552,174	0.841945	1405,071	1682,907	1603,002	1755,869	1988,155	2029,295	1,946,354	1,647,490	1,421,838
80–84	1227,709	0.708507	1306,845	1182,992	1416,915	1349,640	1478,345	1673,917	1,708,555	1,638,723	1,387,095
85–89	857,207	0.522058	869,840	925,909	838,158	1003,894	956,229	1047,417	1,185,982	1,210,523	1,161,046
90–94	407,669	0.304686	447,512	454,107	483,378	437,567	524,091	499,207	546,813	619,152	631,964
95–99	100,547	0.166759	124,211	136,351	138,360	147,279	133,321	159,684	152,102	166,606	188,647
Totale	31,209,230		30,564,931	29,735,949	28,788,653	27,747,879	26,603,851	25,334,226	23,923,284	22,409,884	20,871,475

Source: our elaboration on ISTAT's data.

Table 2a. Female Italian population projected on 1 January.

Age classes	Male 01/01/2016	Px=Lx+s/Lx	Male population projected at the 01-01								
			2021	2026	2031	2036	2041	2046	2051	2056	2061
0–4	1,322,506	0.999388	1,227,872	1,138,837	1,082,305	1,042,681	1,004,104	952,421	888,899	828,593	780,447
5–9	1,469,465	0.999512	1,321,696	1,227,120	1,138,140	1,081,642	1,042,043	1,003,489	951,838	888,355	828,086
10–14	1,469,325	0.998736	1,468,748	1,321,051	1,226,521	1,137,584	1,081,114	1,041,534	1,002,999	951,373	887,921
15–19	1,490,426	0.997456	1,467,467	1,466,891	1,319,381	1,224,970	1,136,146	1,079,747	1,040,217	1,001,731	950,170
20–24	1,563,396	0.997159	1,486,634	1,463,734	1,463,159	1,316,024	1,221,854	1,133,256	1,077,001	1,037,571	999,182
25–29	1,653,304	0.996774	1,558,954	1,482,411	1,459,575	1,459,002	1,312,285	1,218,383	1,130,036	1,073,941	1,034,623
30–34	1,776,419	0.996181	1,647,971	1,553,926	1,477,629	1,454,868	1,454,296	1,308,052	1,214,453	1,126,391	1,070,477
35–39	2,043,171	0.994695	1,769,636	1,641,678	1,547,992	1,471,987	1,449,312	1,448,743	1,303,057	1,209,815	1,122,090
40–44	2,380,558	0.991699	2,032,333	1,760,248	1,632,970	1,539,781	1,464,179	1,441,624	1,441,058	1,296,145	1,203,398
45–49	2,441,662	0.986741	2,360,796	2,015,462	1,745,636	1,619,414	1,526,998	1,452,024	1,429,657	1,429,095	1,285,385
50–54	2,337,449	0.978082	2,409,288	2,329,495	1,988,739	1,722,491	1,597,942	1,506,752	1,432,772	1,410,701	1,410,147
55–59	1,990,139	0.963968	2,286,216	2,356,481	2,278,436	1,945,149	1,684,737	1,562,918	1,473,727	1,401,368	1,379,781
60–64	1,755,003	0.942458	1,918,430	2,203,839	2,271,572	2,196,339	1,875,061	1,624,032	1,506,603	1,420,625	1,350,874
65–69	1,757,419	0.908633	1,654,017	1,808,041	2,077,027	2,140,862	2,069,958	1,767,167	1,530,583	1,419,911	1,338,880
70–74	1,322,775	0.851469	1,596,850	1,502,895	1,642,846	1,887,256	1,945,259	1,880,833	1,605,707	1,390,739	1,290,178
75–79	1,227,379	0.748313	1,126,302	1,359,668	1,279,669	1,398,833	1,606,940	1,656,328	1,601,472	1,367,210	1,184,171
80–84	826,785	0.594712	918,463	842,826	1,017,457	957,593	1,046,765	1,202,494	1,239,452	1,198,402	1,023,101
85–89	448,203	0.418676	491,699	546,221	501,239	605,094	569,492	622,523	715,137	737,117	712,704
90–94	154,221	0.235102	187,652	205,863	228,690	209,857	253,338	238,433	260,636	299,411	308,613
95–99	26,716	0.137514	36,258	44,117	48,399	53,765	49,338	59,560	56,056	61,276	70,392
Total	29,456,321	0.04	28,967,283	28,270,804	27,427,381	26,465,192	25,391,161	24,200,314	22,901,358	21,549,768	20,230,620

Source: our elaboration on ISTAT's data.

Table 2b. Male Italian population projected on 1 January.

http://dx.doi.org/10.5772/67819

Age classes	Population 01/01/2016	Px=Lx+s/Lx	Population projected at the 01-01								
			2021	2026	2031	2036	2041	2046	2051	2056	2061
0–4	2,572,948	0.999474	2,371,377	2,183,009	2,062,889	1,983,557	1,910,569	1,811,050	1,685,135	1,562,890	1,464,532
5–9	2,854,720	0.999615	2,571,481	2,370,023	2,181,762	2,061,711	1,982,424	1,909,477	1,810,015	1,684,172	1,561,997
10–14	2,854,191	0.999399	2,853,469	2,570,354	2,368,984	2,180,804	2,060,805	1,981,552	1,908,638	1,809,220	1,683,431
15–19	2,881,548	0.999078	2,851,502	2,850,780	2,567,933	2,366,747	2,178,739	2,058,849	1,979,671	1,906,826	1,807,502
20–24	3,036,187	0.999053	2,876,473	2,846,492	2,845,772	2,563,425	2,362,577	2,174,887	2,055,199	1,976,158	1,903,443
25–29	3,260,703	0.998796	3,030,350	2,870,933	2,841,023	2,840,305	2,558,504	2,358,025	2,170,681	2,051,213	1,972,321
30–34	3,537,822	0.998214	3,253,435	3,023,550	2,864,479	2,834,652	2,833,936	2,552,771	2,352,723	2,165,783	2,046,572
35–39	4,080,470	0.997132	3,527,893	3,244,274	3,014,991	2,856,360	2,826,632	2,825,918	2,545,553	2,346,053	2,159,625
40–44	4,780,533	0.995115	4,063,790	3,513,463	3,230,970	3,002,573	2,844,582	2,814,994	2,814,284	2,535,078	2,336,377
45–49	4,931,685	0.992087	4,749,047	4,036,995	3,490,286	3,209,608	2,982,645	2,825,684	2,796,318	2,795,613	2,518,265
50–54	4,757,688	0.987580	4,879,608	4,698,847	3,994,275	3,453,336	3,175,553	2,950,880	2,795,562	2,766,548	2,765,851
55–59	4,101,062	0.981367	4,676,397	4,796,120	4,618,362	3,925,778	3,394,085	3,120,936	2,899,919	2,747,232	2,718,789
60–64	3,646,240	0.970783	3,990,020	4,549,483	4,665,753	4,492,666	3,818,785	3,301,530	3,035,590	2,820,243	2,671,661
65–69	3,684,918	0.952879	3,489,998	3,819,105	4,354,138	4,465,092	4,299,193	3,654,101	3,159,069	2,904,225	2,697,606
70–74	2,856,226	0.916280	3,433,523	3,252,363	3,559,147	4,057,068	4,159,969	4,005,024	3,403,727	2,942,489	2,704,551
75–79	2,779,553	0.841945	2,531,373	3,042,576	2,882,672	3,154,702	3,595,096	3,685,623	3,547,826	3,014,700	2,606,010
80–84	2,054,494	0.708507	2,225,308	2,025,819	2,434,373	2,307,233	2,525,109	2,876,411	2,948,006	2,837,125	2,410,197
85–89	1,305,410	0.522058	1,361,539	1,472,130	1,339,397	1,608,988	1,525,721	1,669,941	1,901,119	1,947,639	1,873,750
90–94	561,890	0.304686	635,164	659,970	712,068	647,424	777,430	737,640	807,449	918,563	940,577
95–99	127,263	0.166759	160,469	180,468	186,759	201,044	182,659	219,244	208,158	227,882	259,039
Total	60,665,551		59,532,214	58,006,753	56,216,034	54,213,071	51,995,012	49,534,539	46,824,642	43,959,652	41,102,094

Source: our elaboration on ISTAT's data.

Table 2c. Total population (male + female) projected on 1 January.

It seems obvious that, while talking about projections of such a distant time (2061), at least 40% of the population living at that time is a population that still has to be born; a population that will inevitably bring with them habits, customs, traditions, and ideas that probably have not yet been formed in the current social and political scenarios. This could also mean a different way of facing problems, such as reproductive life, family, and social organization.

At present, moreover, the path of that idea of political unity of Europe would seem less likely: in fact, Europe is struggling to feel truly one people also because of the undeniable, great tradition that distinguishes the individual peoples of Europe.

Certainly, the emergence or not of a strong (social and/or political) movement of restoration of the autonomous economies or the definitive success of the European community project might make it necessary to rewrite the pages of history entirely different from one another, which, although not universally accepted, certainly influence the demographic behavior of the future generations.

A further consideration which is necessary before carrying out the analysis concerns the immigration component, which must not be confused with the foreign component among population (currently) residing in Italy.

More than 4,030,000 foreigners entered the register [11] on 31 December (equal to over 7% of the population): they are regularly included in these calculations and are sufficiently adapted to the behaviors of native population in order to considerably modify therein the future demographic behavior.

On the other hand, the focus here is on the immigrant component that powers our population with an annual balance of about 230,000 foreign nationals resident in Italy (280,000 registrations from abroad against 40,000 cancellations).

This part of the population, without considering that illegal immigration which is by its nature difficult to quantify (and moreover with all attempts to estimate since the 1980s, badly failed), could affect the final results of the projection, but precisely because of absolute randomness, it remains an absolutely uncontrolled portion on which it is more appropriate to make specific ad hoc comments.

Of course, as always, to put forward a hypothesis about values so distant in time may turn out to be a scientific quirk rather than a real possibility of analysis, because, in any case, any method utilized may return plausible values only, ignoring, de facto, possible major shifts in socio-demographic behavior of the population.

In any case, in light of these premises, the projection of the population was made under the assumption, as already mentioned, that it is closed and so made in the absence of migratory movements. This choice, not made randomly, really intends to answer the initial assumption, which turns out to be: what would happen to the future generations of workers if the population were projected as it is in the future?

That is, to be more precise, what situation would be created to the relationship between outgoing generations and incoming generations in the labor market, if this demographic situation persisted?

The analysis, then, was carried out by building quinquennial projections between 2016 and 2061, a time when the strength of the generations born in the baby boom (and living boom) era should have exhausted, and that at that date they should be really residual by then from the quantitative point of view.

The projections, built with the standard method, have been built for five-year periods, so they are available every five years from 2016 to 2061, but for the obvious need for space, only some significant years that are functional to the initial hypothesis are reported here.

Reaffirming once again the weakness of precision resulting from having fixed, inexorably, the law of mortality and the law of current fertility, under the assumption that they be unchanged for the next half century (not entirely appropriate assumption, but not too dissimilar from reality, except for some small correction factors), the results of elaboration return values open to interesting considerations.

First, the wave of those born in the baby boom era is now coming to the end of the race. In 2061, only very few representatives of this "era" will still be alive, leaving behind them much

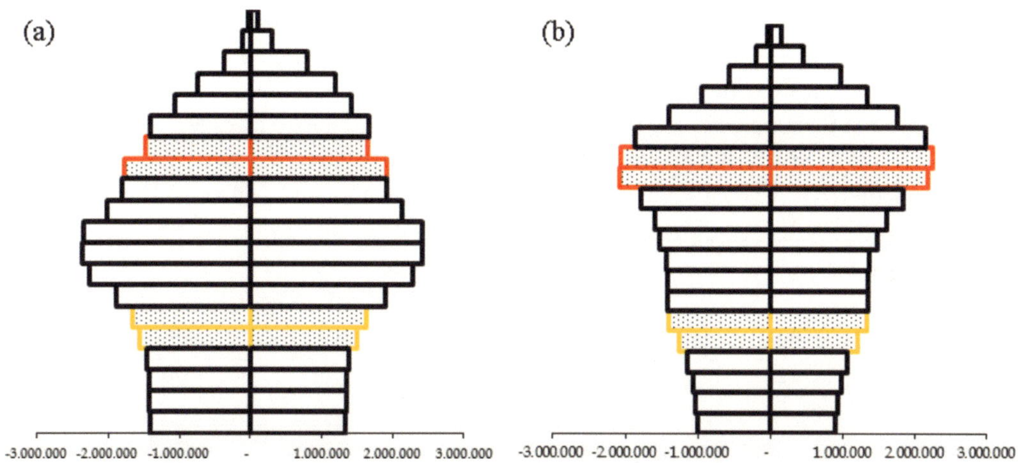

Figure 3. (a) Pyramid of Italian population, 2016. Source: our elaboration on ISTAT's data; (b) pyramid of Italian population, 2041. Source: our elaboration on ISTAT's data.

less consistent generations. These generations, although saved certainly by survival rates,[5] are, at the individual age, better than those that preceded them, will not be able to "replace" the generations of their predecessors. In simple terms, the Italian population is destined to decline

[5]The survival rate expresses in relative terms how many people belonging to the current age will reach the next one. In scientific terms: $px = (L_{x+s})/L_x$.

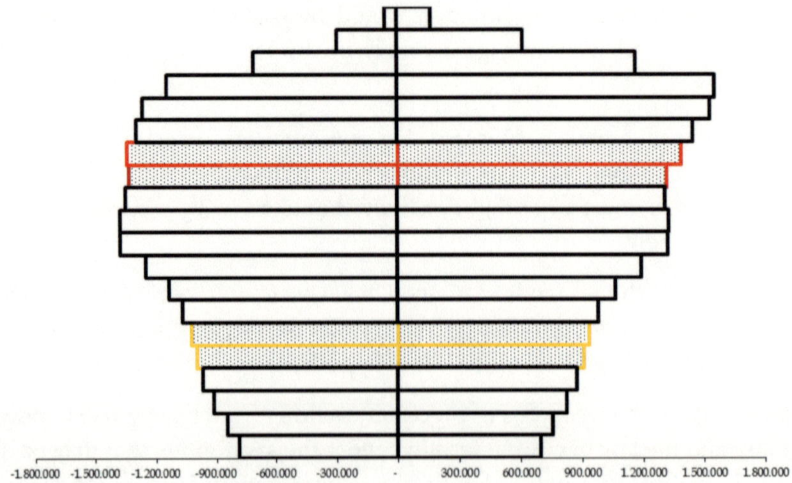

Figure 4. Pyramid of Italian population, 2061. Source: our elaboration on ISTAT's data.

substantially, starting already from the next few years with peaks of decline in the next two decades.

This situation is not only accompanied by the quantitative downsizing but will also reshape the population structure itself. In other words, the graphic representation of the population by age groups will hardly continue to be indicated as the "age pyramid" according to the data that will present themselves as a future scenario; it will rather have to be called the population "barrel" by age to reach, not so much time afterwards, the "inverted pyramid," where, for many years, (all those years for which the "baby-living-boom" lasted) the top of the graph will

Age groups	Years					
	2016	2041	2046	2051	2056	2061
0–20	18.40	15.64	15.67	15.77	15.84	15.86
65+	22.04	32.82	34.01	34.12	33.65	32.82
80+	6.67	9.64	11.11	12.52	13.49	13.34

Source: our elaboration on ISTAT's data.

Table 3. Percentage of population in age groups, Italy.

be much bigger than its bottom (despite in the presence of a slight recovery of women's fertility, which will, however, not be supported by an appropriate quantity of women available for procreation) [1].[6]

[6]Basically, as stated, the fertility rate will return increasing values due to the mother "in late" fertility recovery (35 years old and more); but the total of women in the age group available to procreate will be more bounded in the previous group, nullifying the effects of the improvement in the procreation propensity.

http://dx.doi.org/10.5772/67819

To confirm what has just been mentioned above, it is enough to observe what is shown in **Figures 2** and **3a** and **b**, which draw the age "pyramids" of the Italian population in 2016, 2041 (i.e., a quarter of century later), and 2061 (**Figure 4**, 45 years later) and in **Tables 2a–c**, which show the amount of the projections of the closed population, calculated from 2021 to 2061.

5. The health of industrialized populations

A major problem, which certainly will be faced in the coming decades, will be caused by the progressive aging of the population in all more developed countries and will reach very significant proportions particularly in Italy (**Table 3**).

In Italy, for example, around 2050, more than a third of the population will be over 65-year-old and a third of these will be over 80 years.

An important consideration, however, is that despite the generations that will overlook the threshold of the 80 years from 2050 will come from generations born in the late twentieth century, when, then, they had already a culture of health, the knowledge that styles correct and adequate life can improve the quality of life, especially by the elderly, massive campaigns against smoking and use of drugs, certainly the frightening growth of older age groups will pose new structural limits to the population [12].

It is undeniable, in fact, that a large amount of pathologies that are spreading in recent years are closely related to age, and the growth of this will not only bring with it the growth and spread of diseases today marginal if not, indeed, unknown.

This lot will commit the future governance, on the identification of resources to cope with this situation and the migratory flows in the next few decades could be the key to restore vitality to a population particularly in trouble [13].

Author details

Pietro Iaquinta

Address all correspondence to: pietro.iaquinta@unical.it

University of Calabria, Rende, Italy

References

[1] Livi Bacci M. Storia minima della popolazione del Mondo. Bologna: Il Mulino; 2011

[2] Salvini S, De Rose A. Rapporto sulla popolazione. L'Italia a 150 dall'Unità. Bologna: Il Mulino; 2011

[3] Iaquinta P, Traversa T. Evoluzione della fecondità nelle società post-transizionali. The Paper Presented at the Giornate di Studio della Popolazione; 20–22 February 2001; Milano

[4] Iaquinta P. La fecondità in Italia. Integrazione ed omogeneizzazione dei dati con modellistica ARIMA. In: Da Molin G, editor. Prospettive di ricerca. Book series "Saggi e Ricerche". n. 34, Bari: Department of Historical and Geographical; 2003

[5] Iaquinta P. Some consideration about fertility in Italy: Methodological problems. International Area Review. Vol. 6, N. 2. Korea: Hankuk University of Foreign Studies; 2003

[6] ISTAT. Serie Storiche, L'archivio della Statistica Italiana. Datawarehause on-line; 2017

[7] Iaquinta P. Crisi di mortalità: il contributo delle interruzioni volontarie di gravidanza. In: Helzel PB, Katolo AJ, editors. Autorità e crisi dei poteri. Padova: Cedam; 2012

[8] Billari FC, Della Zuanna G. La rivoluzione della cultura. Il declino che non c'è. Milano: Università Bocconi Editore; 2008

[9] ISTAT. La popolazione in cifre. demo.istat.it/popolazione per età; 2017

[10] ISTAT. La fecondità in Italia. Datawarehause; 2017

[11] ISTAT. Stranieri in Italia. La popolazione straniera residente in Italia. Report Statistiche. Comunicato Stampa; 2016

[12] Iaquinta P, Da Molin G, Fiore F, Sabella E. Il turnover di popolazione disponibile al lavoro. Vol. 68. Roma: Rivista SIEDS; 2014

[13] Stranges M. L'invecchiamento demografico in Italia: Verso un miglioramento della relazione tra età e lavoro. Quaderni Europei sul nuovo Welfare. 2007;7:102–118

Other important references

[1] Alietti A, Agustoni A, editors. Integrazione, casa e immigrazione. Esperienze e prospettive in Europa. Italia e Lombardia. Milano: Fondazione ISMU; 2013

[2] Altavilla AM, Galizia F, Mazza A. Indicatori di carico demografico ed invecchiamento della popolazione. Rivista Italiana di Economia Demografia e Statistica; 2012

[3] Baldi S, Cagiano De Azevedo R. La Popolazione Italiana, storia demografica dal dopoguerra ad oggi. Il Mulino; 2005

[4] Cesareo V, Blangiardo GC, editors. Integration Indexes. An Empirical Research on Migration in Italy. Milano: Fondazione ISMU; 2011

[5] Coleman D. Immigration and Ethnic Change in Low-Fertility Countries: A Third Demographic Transition. Population and Development Review. n. 3. 2006

[6] Feltri S. Recessione, la peggiore della storia d'Italia. Il Fatto Quotidiano; 2012

[7] Fondazione ISMU. XX rapporto sulle Migrazioni. Milano: Franco Angeli; 2014

[8] Iaquinta P. Implicazioni demografiche sull'evoluzione del mercato del lavoro in provincia di Bari. Atti del convegno: Ambiente, salute e qualità della vita del; 2005

[9] ISTAT. Il futuro demografico del Paese, previsioni regionali della popolazione residente al 2065. Press release of 28/12/2011

[10] ISTAT. La Popolazione Straniera Residente in Italia, 01/01/2011. Press release of 22/09/2011

[11] ISTAT. Natalità e Fecondità della Popolazione Residente 2011. Press release of 14/11/2012

[12] ISTAT. 15° Censimento generale della popolazione e delle abitazioni 9 ottobre 2011, Struttura demografica della popolazione, dati definitive; 2012

[13] ISTAT. Il Censimento della Popolazione Straniera; 19/12/2012

[14] ISTAT. Bilancio Demografico Nazionale: Popolazione residente, natalità, mortalità, migrazioni, famiglie e convivenze. Press release years various

[15] ISTAT. Occupati e disoccupati, dati ricostruiti dal 1977. Press release of 24/04/2013

[16] ISTAT, INPS. Trattamenti Pensionistici e Beneficiari, Anno 2011. Press release of 17/04/2013

[17] Livi Bacci M. (a cura). Demografia del capitale umano. Bologna: Il Mulino; 2010

[18] Sobotka T. Is lowest-low fertility in Europe explained by the postponement of childbearing? Population and Development Review. 2004:2

[19] Sperotti F. Demografia e mercato del lavoro: i cambiamenti dei prossimi quarant'anni. Milano Giuffrè: Editore; 2011

[20] Zenezini M. Invecchiamento della popolazione crescita, occupazione. Studi e Note di Economia. Anno XIV. 2009;3:431–468

Chapter 3

Extending Health Information System Evaluation with an Importance-Performance Map Analysis

Mohd Idzwan Mohd Salleh, Rosni Abdullah and
Nasriah Zakaria

Additional information is available at the end of the chapter

http://dx.doi.org/10.5772/68122

Abstract

Evaluation of a health information system is necessary for determining effective use and for enhancing the productivity of medical practitioners. However, the current system evaluation toolkit does not recommend specific areas required for further improvement. The objective of this chapter was to identify those constructs and their attributes that were the most suitable candidates for managerial intervention by applying partial least squares structural equation modeling. In doing so, the quantitative survey was adopted from the past studies together with new items creation representing system quality, records quality, service quality, and knowledge quality as the predictors while effective use and user performance as the outcomes. When extending the findings in importance-performance map analysis, two-system quality attributes (workflows fit and work styles fit) and all-knowledge quality attributes exhibited higher importance rank for managerial actions. The chapter also provides a valuable recommendation for the policy and decision-makers at the managerial level on how to apply the proposed system evaluation method in producing more efficient strategic-planning strategies for further system upgrades and new implementation at health facilities.

Keywords: summative evaluation, health information system, effectiveness, partial least squares structural equation modeling, importance-performance map analysis

1. Introduction

The widespread implementation and adoption of health information systems (HISs) around the world are believed to improve access and use of health data in ensuring high quality of care and health system efficiency and fostering clinical research [1, 2]. The acceleration of HIS implementations will further enhance sharing of health information electronically across different clinical settings [3] that eventually generate quality benefits and minimize medical costs from avoiding unnecessary clinical trials, examinations, and treatments [4]. Therefore, the management and presentation of HISs are vital to accelerate patient care and its continuity across health institutions [5]. The success of system implementation relies upon a high quality of information outputs from HISs required to make timely and accurate clinical decisions by various health practitioners [6]. Besides enabling care continuity, HIS is regarded as the wealthiest source of clinical evidence to support continuous communication among individual clinicians and surgical team works [7]. With the use of HIS, it is not only capable to reduce human errors [8] but also contributes to an increased adherence to clinical guidelines and deterrence of medical errors [9, 10], thereby delivering greater patient safety and medication management [11].

In Malaysia, the expenditures of customized HISs are fully supported by the government in the efforts to retain a higher standard of patient care [12, 13]. All new public hospitals should be equipped with HISs designed from multiple vendors hired by the government. Although the investment of IS can improve health service, it will also present more costs in maintenance, hardware replacements, end-user trainings, and system upgrades [14, 15]. Increasing medical costs [16] and enormous budget cuts among local hospitals have demanded for a comprehensive evaluation of HIS to investigate the most possible strengths and weaknesses for further improvements. In reality, the effectiveness of HIS adoption among implemented government hospitals had never been assessed since its first kick-off at Selayang Hospital in 1999. Hospitals with HISs are repeatedly distributing user satisfaction surveys without concentrating on significant success factors and impact on the performance of the health personnel. They conducted these surveys to satisfy the auditing needs but the results were still insufficient in recommending which critical attributes for improving system use and user productivity. As a consequence, the government hospitals were still incapable of choosing the right HIS and vendors and even assessing its performance after implementation [17]. A systematic IS evaluation will not only promote efficient use and medical cost savings but also cope with unresolved issues of clinicians' heavy workloads and shortage of specialists in this multi-racial country [14, 15].

Identifying the needs of health workforce and acknowledging the characteristics of HIS are essential to their productivity that must be emphasized in any evaluation studies [18, 19]. For that reason, recognizing the main attributes of HIS can improve health practitioners' performance from their daily use. Strategies to upgrade an HIS could not precede with an absence of in-depth knowledge about the most significant HIS characteristics in predicting user productivity. Consequently, there will be wasted expenses on any system upgrades without careful understanding of the potential system impacts or benefits to the user performance, thereby introducing dissatisfaction and risks of system failure [18].

Unfortunately, there is little evidence on the prior HIS research in measuring the influence of IS attributes toward satisfaction and productivity of medical practitioners [20, 21]. Besides, the previous evaluation works did not completely assess the importance and performance of multiple HIS attributes especially in ranking those attributes with high importance for managerial attention. There are only two current studies attempted to prioritize different HIS quality measures among small samples acquired in one public hospital [18, 19]. Furthermore, the current trends in examining HIS use and user satisfaction in the scholarly publications are still plenty by ignoring core success drivers that will predict user and organizational impacts. By contrast, there are many empirical studies on HIS evaluation concerning the effects of system quality, information quality, service quality, usage, user satisfaction, and net benefits in the developed and developing countries [22, 23], but none of them address on the critical quality or success factors required for managerial response. Most studies only present significant results without recommending specific measures or indicators that will guide the hospitals in prioritizing the most important indicators for improving effective use and health personnel productivity.

2. Conceptual foundation

The DeLone and McLean IS success models (DMISMs) are the most outstanding theoretical frameworks adopted by IS researchers since the past two decades for IS evaluation including the health-care domain [22, 23]. The models embrace system quality, information quality, service quality, actual use, and user satisfaction to predict individual impact, organizational impact, and net benefits [24, 25]. In our empirical study, the traditional DMISM models will be extended to incorporate knowledge quality and effective use in predicting individual performance based on the perception of medical practitioners as HIS system users.

2.1. Effective use and user performance

Effective use and user performance are the two outcome constructs measured in our evaluation study. When actual system use denotes the extent or frequency of HIS usage [26], effective use more refers to the outputs of HIS usage that allows the medical practitioners to complete their clinical tasks easily without any misdiagnosis and inaccurate medication. Because of the mandatory use of HIS, the actual use remains unreliable in assessing IS success [27, 28].

Previous research indicated that user satisfaction had a strong relationship with system quality, information quality, and individual impact [29, 30]. This construct is indeed composed of system quality and individual impact measures [31] that finally disclosed a little explanatory power [32]. Consequently, user satisfaction is omitted as the outcome construct in the study.

On the other hand, individual impact is the outcome generated by IS workers from their applied IT knowledge, skills, and experiences [33]. Likewise, user performance in this study refers to the level to which the practitioners gain benefits from the effective use of HIS by considering patient care and safety, work productivity, and performance score.

2.2. Predictors of health information system evaluation

System quality is the attributes or characteristics of HIS including functionality, features, interface design, and its performance to facilitate ease of clinical task completion [34]. With regard to past empirical studies on the most important predictors of HIS quality [19, 22, 23, 35], we will limit the scope of measuring this predictor with the four measures namely adequate IT infrastructure, system interoperability, perceived security concerns, and system compatibility.

In the conventional DMISMs, information quality describes the usable, meaningful, and understanding the content and format of IS outputs [24, 36]. Clinicians can deliver the right care depending on the quality of information produced from HIS [37]. For that reason, successful adoption of HIS is determined from the quality of records it produced [7]. The researchers will more specify the generic term of information quality with records quality based on timely access, consistency, standardized, accuracy, duplication prevention, and completeness of patient notes, reports, prescriptions, images, laboratory test results, and discharge summaries.

In general, service quality is about the type of IS support delivered by the responsible IS providers or personnel [38]. We will extend service quality construct with quick assistance, problem-solving capability, follow-up service, and adequate training in the study.

The advancement of interoperable HISs from time to time will not only create, store, and manage data and information but also knowledge [12, 35]. The aim of HIS adoption in most hospitals is to acquire, classify, store, access, and simplify the use of knowledge from a HIS repository of patient health information for supporting clinical decision-making, actions, and problem solving [39, 40]. Besides, HISs can be utilized to promote knowledge management activities in a health organization through medical research and education [41]. In essence, medical knowledge is classified into two types such as tacit and explicit. Tacit knowledge is gathered through professional practices and experiences of medical practitioners while explicit knowledge is generally embedded and presented into the forms of electronic health records (EHRs), electronic medical records (EMRs), clinicians' workflows, clinical guidelines, and protocols [42, 43]. HIS also integrates clinical decision support system (CDSS) and computerized provider order entry (CPOE) as the knowledge tools to hold medical knowledge [39, 42–44]. It should be noted that the wide adoption of HIS worldwide is not only due to EHRs but also its integration with CDSS and CPOE to raise higher quality of patient care [45]. Hence, the quality of knowledge must be included in any HIS evaluation [12, 41]. As a new measuring predictor in this study, knowledge quality is defined as the level to which the medical practitioners believe that using HIS will increase their medical knowledge and competencies [41] and then practice it to deliver the best patient care.

3. Empirical example

Our study would bridge the knowledge gap with current empirical proof in the local health system to determine the importance and performance of several effectiveness factors for immediate managerial actions with regard to the effective use of HISs and medical practitioners' performance as the measuring outcomes. The research design would employ a quantitative method with the distribution of survey questionnaire to the four groups of health personnel in the three different government hospitals with multiple HISs. By utilizing importance-performance map analysis (IPMA) feature in partial least squares structural equation modeling (PLS-SEM), the expected outcomes could establish the most critical quality attributes for effective use and user performance improvements.

An ethic approval was obtained from the Medical Research and Ethics Committee Malaysia as the study engaged the human subject responses from varying clinical professionals. Subsequently, the data were gathered from three hospitals situated in different states with different HIS packages. These hospitals had more than 1000 health personnel with more than 500 beds for patients. Specifically, Kedah Hospital used iSOFT system, Pahang Hospital used F1S1C1EN® system, and Johor Hospital used Cerner system. Connected via a centralized and secured 1Gov*Net network, all HISs are integrated with various clinical modules including patient management, laboratory, radiology, pharmacy, picture archiving and communication, nursing, and operating theater management. The implemented systems are in the current phase of operation and maintenance while the contract is renewed for every 3 years. The government did not standardize the use of single HIS package across their administered hospitals in order to avoid monopoly by a sole vendor that will render a negative image to the public.

Adopted from past surveys [36, 38, 41, 46–50] with 19 new item additions anchoring by seven-point Likert scales from 1 of strongly disagree to 7 of strongly agree, the questionnaire draft was proven valid and reliable after pretesting between key HIS experts and pilot testing among 100 samples of end users using exploratory factor analysis in statistical package for social science (SPSS) software. The field survey data contained 888 samples from specialists, medical officers, and nursing staffs collected by the mean of convenience sampling technique. Overall, 353 participated respondents were from Kedah Hospital, 213 from Pahang Hospital, and 322 respondents from Johor Hospital. Specifically, 71 and 96 were specialists and assistant medical officers, respectively, 328 were medical officers, and 393 were nurses. More than 70% of respondents were female due to imbalance recruitments of clinical professionals and nurses were majorly female while 64% of total samples aged between 25 and 35 years old. About 53% of assistant medical officers and nurses had Diploma qualifications in medical and nursing, respectively, whereas the remaining 47% medical officers and specialists had Bachelor, Masters, or PhD Degree in medical.

The collected data were subjected to confirmatory factor analysis using SmartPLS software. In this study, system quality characteristics namely adequate IT infrastructure, system interoperability, perceived security concerns, and system compatibility are identified as the formative measures. The formative model exhibited no collinearity issue for all measuring indicators and passed weight significance at a level of 1%. Then, in the reflective model, all question items satisfy the required outer loadings, composite reliability (CR), and average variance extracted (AVE) scores above the suggested thresholds [51, 52], confirming the convergent validity. However, one attribute of knowledge quality (knowqual_4) was deleted due to lower factor loading below 0.70.

Discriminant validity was then executed using the Fornell and Larcker [53] criterion, and cross-loading methods. Every construct average variance extracted is more than 0.50 that satisfied the required criterion [53, 54] while cross-loading scores of bolded indicators are higher than its opposing indicators in other constructs [55].

The next assessment was preceded to evaluate the path model. After running a complete bootstrapping test with 5000 subsamples and no sign option setting, the PLS results in **Table 1** demonstrate that the observed path coefficients were statistically significant at either 0.05 or 0.01

	(effective use) *R*-squared: 0.260	Path coefficients (user performance) *R*-squared: 0.640
System quality	0.320 (6.025***)	0.122 (3.127***)
Records quality	0.103 (2.115**)	0.137 (3.515***)
Service quality	0.047 (1.244)	0.139 (4.632***)
Knowledge quality	0.121 (2.520**)	0.489 (12.464***)
Effective use	-	0.104 (4.170***)

Significance Level: ***$p < 0.01$, **$p < 0.05$.

Table 1. Path coefficients.

level, and had positive effects on the outcomes or target constructs except for service quality and effective use relationships. The outcome of user performance had the largest predictive power explained by quality predictors and effective use. More importantly, knowledge quality as a new predictor became the strongest predictor for user performance at a 1% level of significance. This construct also had large effect size among other predictors that justified a need for measuring knowledge quality in future system evaluation studies.

The path coefficient scores for each latent construct would be subjected to further assessment in importance-performance map analysis. IPMA in PLS-SEM adopts the traditional IPA method in ranking both critical constructs and their measured indicators' importance and performance for managerial intervention [51, 56]. Moreover, PLS-SEM simplifies the researchers to model both higher-order constructs and their individual indicators simultaneously for calculating attribute importance scores. It helps to reduce the collinearity issues between the attribute items if using a simple regression analysis [57]. The study results can be valuable in contributing to the practical implications to decision-makers and administrators by incorporating IPMA. IPMA extends the PLS-SEM results for path coefficient scores by contrasting the total effects of constructs' importance in measuring target constructs with their average latent scores representing their performance.

In a graphical representation, IPMA contrasts the (unstandardized) total effects on the horizontal axis with the latent construct scores, rating on a scale of 0–100, on the vertical axis. The estimated results will be emphasized on the bottom of IPMA diagram [58]. The key objective of this analysis is to improve the performance of constructs with greater importance (strong total effect) but lower performance (small construct score) in predicting a single or more target constructs [51, 55]. Hence, the subsequent analysis would apply IPMA to highlight which latent constructs and their manifest attributes necessary for remedial attentions by both decision-makers and hospital administrators.

The IPMA diagram in **Figure 1** exhibits system quality has the strongest total effect over the outcome construct. Consequently, knowledge quality, records quality, and service quality should be improved to increase the effective use of HISs.

When selecting user performance as a target construct as displayed in **Figure 2**, knowledge quality becomes the highest importance among others. System quality, records quality, service quality, and effective use are deserved for critical managerial attention to enhance the performance of medical practitioners. No underperforming construct below 50% is identified.

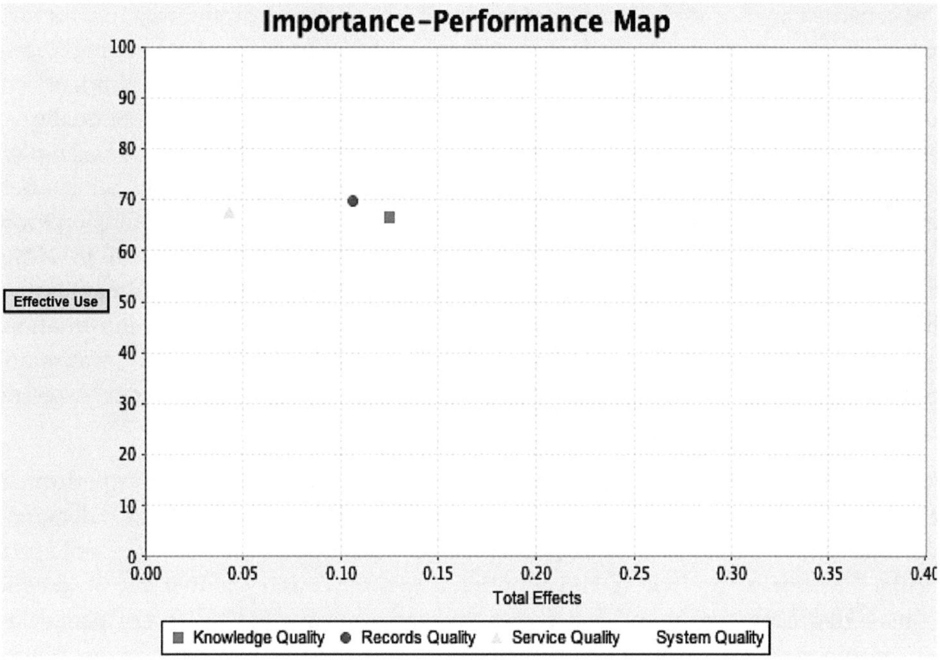

Figure 1. IPMA for effective use at construct level.

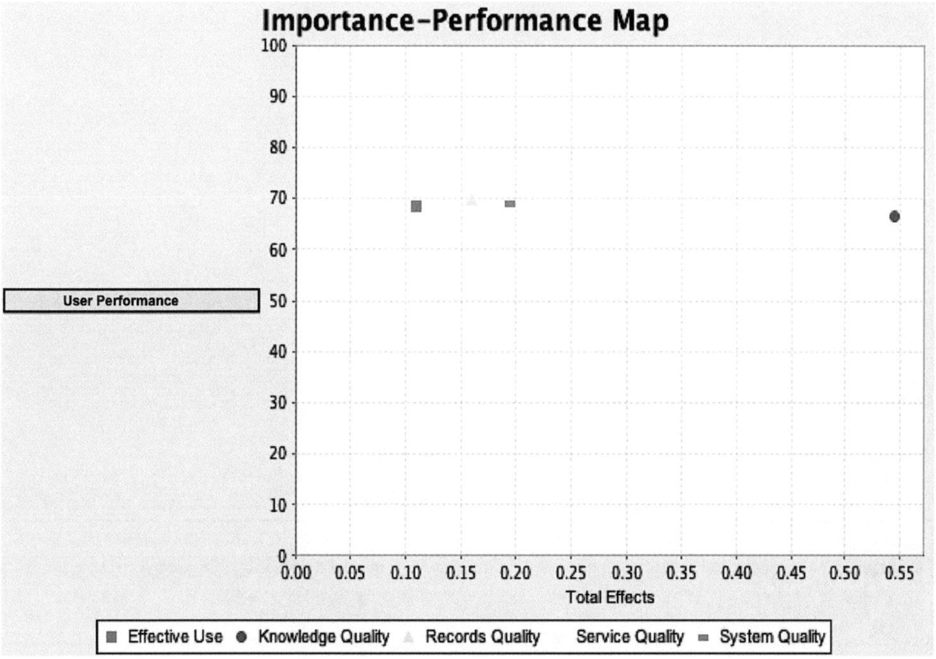

Figure 2. IPMA for user performance at construct level.

As this construct level of analysis does not reveal which specific attributes required for further improvement, a subsequent analysis is continued with the individual measuring items for each latent construct. In **Figure 3**, syscom_1 (workflows fit) and syscom_2 (work styles fit) should be maintained for the continued effective use of HISs. By contrast, other quality attributes that fall into low performance must be stressed for managerial actions. For example, the attribute secc_4 (secure and save) has an average importance on effective use, while offering room for improving its performance. IT departments can focus on offering hands-on training to educate HIS users about securing their access when using the systems [18]. In addition, user access control policy should be enforced and applied across the government hospitals with HISs to prevent unauthorized access and misuse of patient health information by non-responsible doctors. Unfortunately, secc_1 (unauthorized access) attribute was removed from the analysis due to negative outer weight score in the measurement model assessment as suggested by Ringle and Sarstedt [58].

Next, in **Figure 4**, by retaining knowledge quality for sustaining greater user performance, all effective use, service quality, system quality, and records quality attributes demand for urgent intervention. For instance, indicator effuse_2 (misdiagnosis prevention) should receive particular attention by promoting HIS adoption across the country so that any misdiagnosis will be averted from timely and full access to comprehensive EHR of every patient. As a result, the importance of effective use increases and then improves user performance outcome. Interestingly, no attribute falls into the bottom zone, signifying that all measuring items for every predictor achieved more than 60% of performance score in the diagram.

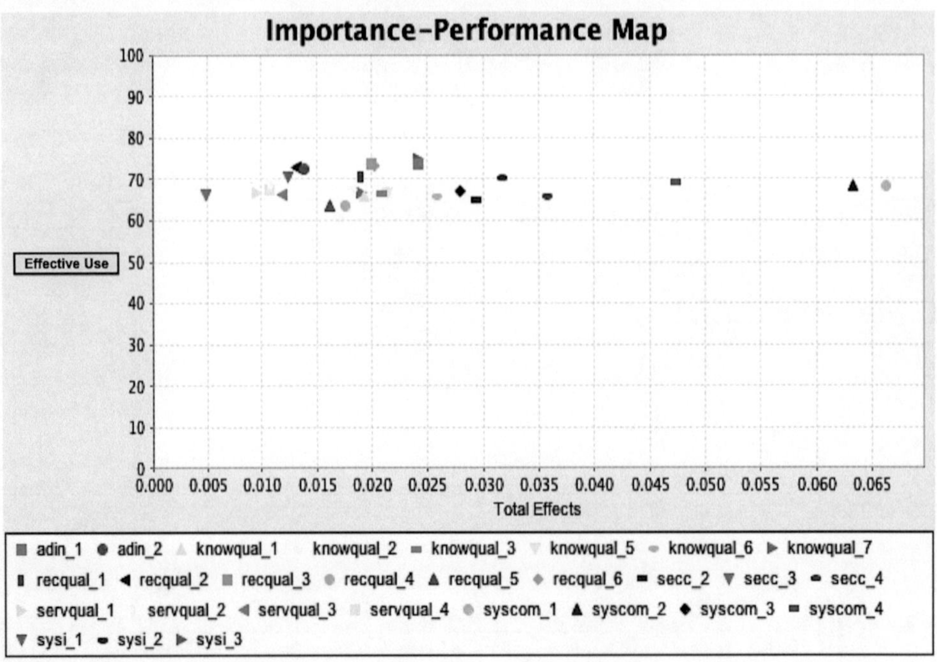

Figure 3. IPMA for effective use at indicator level.

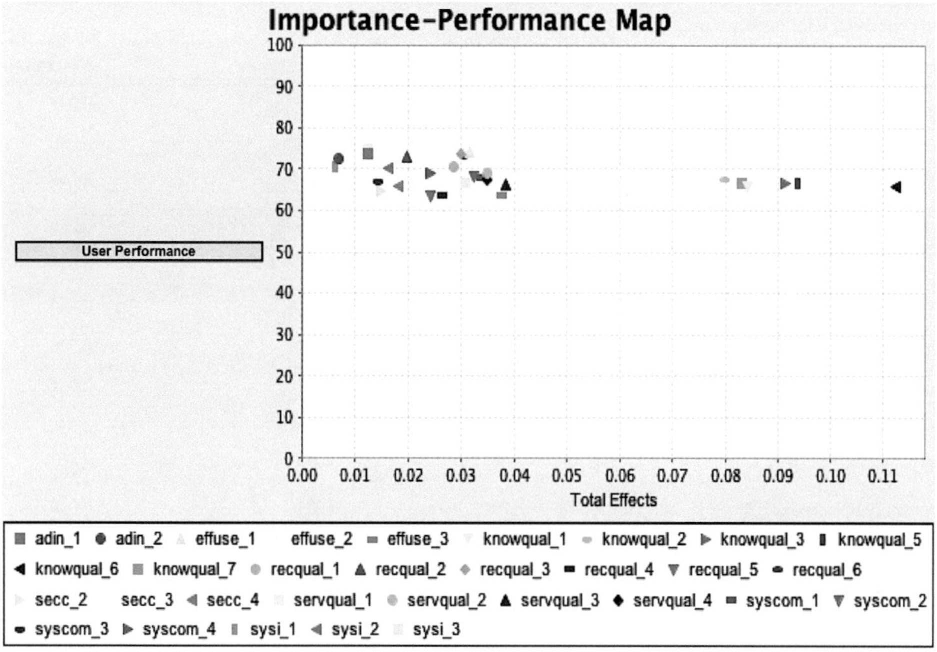

Figure 4. IPMA for user performance at indicator level.

More specifically, **Table 2** lists the importance and performance scores for every predictor attribute with its discrepancy, calculating by subtracting performance value against importance value [59, 60]. In doing so, performance score in percentage of individual attribute has to be converted into three decimal places before computation. The results confirmed that attribute secc_3 (robust security control) of the largest discrepancy in effective use warranted for immediate managerial intervention mainly when the respondents expressed their concerns over lack of security control in HISs. When referring to previous IPMA diagram, this attribute had the lowest total effect (importance) score. Again, a proper security policy must be in place

Target construct: user performance			
Attribute (question item)	**Performance**	**Importance**	**Discrepancy**
Faster network (adin_1)	0.074	0.024	0.050
Adequate computers (adin_2)	0.072	0.014	0.058
Learning of knowledge (knowqual_1)	0.066	0.019	0.047
Researching of knowledge (knowqual_2)	0.067	0.018	0.049
Applying of knowledge (knowqual_3)	0.067	0.021	0.046
Decision-making capability (knowqual_5)	0.067	0.022	0.045
Problem-solving capability (knowqual_6)	0.066	0.026	0.040
Complete medical source (knowqual_7)	0.067	0.019	0.048

Target construct: user performance			
Attribute (question item)	**Performance**	**Importance**	**Discrepancy**
Timely access (recqual_1)	0.070	0.019	0.051
Records consistency (recqual_2)	0.073	0.013	0.060
Standardized format (recqual_3)	0.074	0.020	0.054
Records accuracy (recqual_4)	0.064	0.018	0.046
Repeated tests prevention (recqual_5)	0.063	0.016	0.047
Records completeness (recqual_6)	0.073	0.020	0.053
Data protection (secc_2)	0.065	0.029	0.036
Robust security control (secc_3)	0.066	0.005	0.061
Secure and safe (secc_4)	0.066	0.036	0.030
Quick assistance (servqual_1)	0.067	0.010	0.057
Problem solver (servqual_2)	0.069	0.011	0.058
Follow-up service (servqual_3)	0.066	0.012	0.054
Adequate training (servqual_4)	0.068	0.011	0.057
Workflows fit (syscom_1)	0.068	0.066	0.002
Work styles fit (syscom_2)	0.068	0.063	0.005
Clinical practices fit (syscom_3)	0.067	0.028	0.039
Patient needs fit (syscom_4)	0.069	0.047	0.022
Interoperable systems (sysi_1)	0.070	0.012	0.058
Treatment cost reduction (sysi_2)	0.070	0.032	0.038
Coordinated care (sysi_3)	0.075	0.024	0.051
Target construct: user performance			
Faster network (adin_1)	0.074	0.012	0.062
Adequate computers (adin_2)	0.072	0.007	0.065
Ease of task completion (effuse_1)	0.074	0.032	0.042
Misdiagnosis prevention (effuse_2)	0.068	0.040	0.028
Right medication (effuse_3)	0.064	0.038	0.026
Learning of knowledge (knowqual_1)	0.066	0.084	-0.018
Researching of knowledge (knowqual_2)	0.067	0.080	-0.013
Applying of knowledge (knowqual_3)	0.067	0.091	-0.024
Decision-making capability (knowqual_5)	0.067	0.094	-0.027
Problem-solving capability (knowqual_6)	0.066	0.112	-0.046
Complete medical source (knowqual_7)	0.067	0.083	-0.016
Timely access (recqual_1)	0.070	0.029	0.041
Records consistency (recqual_2)	0.073	0.020	0.053
Standardized format (recqual_3)	0.074	0.030	0.044

Target construct: user performance			
Attribute (question item)	**Performance**	**Importance**	**Discrepancy**
Records accuracy (recqual_4)	0.064	0.026	0.038
Repeated tests prevention (recqual_5)	0.063	0.024	0.039
Records completeness (recqual_6)	0.073	0.031	0.042
Data protection (secc_2)	0.065	0.015	0.050
Robust security control (secc_3)	0.066	0.003	0.063
Secure and safe (secc_4)	0.066	0.018	0.048
Quick assistance (servqual_1)	0.067	0.031	0.036
Problem solver (servqual_2)	0.069	0.035	0.034
Follow-up service (servqual_3)	0.066	0.039	0.027
Adequate training (servqual_4)	0.068	0.035	0.033
Workflows fit (syscom_1)	0.068	0.034	0.034
Work styles fit (syscom_2)	0.068	0.032	0.036
Clinical practices fit (syscom_3)	0.067	0.014	0.053
Patient needs fit (syscom_4)	0.069	0.024	0.045
Interoperable systems (sysi_1)	0.070	0.006	0.064
Treatment cost reduction (sysi_2)	0.070	0.016	0.054
Coordinated care (sysi_3)	0.075	0.012	0.063

Table 2. Performance and importance scores for individual attribute.

to limit the access level by specific clinical roles. Regular monitoring and reporting of access activities can be further improved with audit trail feature. On-site training can be emphasized on instructing users by changing passwords frequently with a combination of numbers, alphabets, and symbols as well as securing their accounts through routine check of logging off after using the systems. By contrast, attribute adin_2 (adequate computers) had the highest discrepancy in user performance outcome, demanding for more computers to use HISs. In coping with a tight budget facing by most hospitals and the increasing rates of doctors, the hospitals may consider to provide grants in purchasing high-performance desktop and laptop computers at low costs from their contracted system vendors.

4. Recommendations for improving system effectiveness at minimal cost

4.1. HIS scorecard

Unfortunately, the Ministry and hospitals in Malaysia did not perform strategic planning in the design, implementation, and upgrade of the HISs. In fact, the future direction of the Ministry is to develop HIS product for extending the system to other hospitals. At present, they are only focused on delivering maintenance services and operational support to existing HISs to ensure uninterrupted hospital services. These services will be continued until a new in-house system is entirely designed and deployed in all IT hospitals. So far, the selected vendor has been initiating the plan for HIS development and implementation, while the Ministry has been the sole licensed user of the product.

In addressing the gaps through proper strategic planning in order to achieve effective use and enhanced user performance objectives, the balanced scorecard (BSC) framework, designated as HIS scorecard (**Figure 5**), is extended on the basis of the applicability of the empirical study results that is highly recommended for the Ministry and IT hospitals. The scorecard is designed by extracting the key results from the IPMA on the basis of the importance scores of the estimated constructs at the indicator level of the analysis. With this scorecard, the respective parties can focus on the development of concrete goals and strategies from validated evidence-based findings for the planning and evaluation of the system implementation rather than on the initiation of a new BSC template. More importantly, it can serve two central purposes:

- As a metric for the policymakers at the Ministry level that facilitates effective decisions concerning the expenditures of HISs in new hospitals or upgrading the current ones. In this regard, the team implementing HIS must define their specific, measurable, achievable, realistic, and time-frame (SMART) actions in order to achieve high effectiveness in their goal concerning predefined system quality, records quality, service quality, knowledge quality, and effective use indicators. After all actions for each strategy have been undertaken, the hospital management will present the completed scorecard with the assistance of the implementing team in front of the Board of Directors of the Ministry during the annual strategic plan meeting. Thus, HIS scorecard can be a significant measurable indicator to guide the strategic direction and the objectives of the national health technology investments in the present and future.
- As a performance measurement for the auditors that assess whether or not the implemented HIS in a single IT hospital is effective. Specifically, it serves as a checklist that determines whether the previous actionable plans are well executed. The next session will further explain on how to execute simple evaluation survey using a concise guideline.

Consequently, the transformation of the study findings into a measurable scorecard will empower the hospital administrators and decision-makers, thus facilitating their thorough understanding on how the performance of HISs positively influences their strategic decision-making through systematic monitoring and increased effective use. Thus, it may contribute to adequate governance because of increased quality of patient care, and facilitates the efficient or prudent use of government budgets.

4.2. Concise HIS effectiveness guideline

In acquiring the inputs for every indicator in the scorecard, we have developed simple ways to evaluate the effectiveness of HIS by proposing "Easy Guide to Efficiently Evaluate Your HIS" in the form of flowchart diagram (see **Figure 6**) for practitioners. The subsequent steps are described as follows:

- Collect the surveys using a validated questionnaire (see Appendix A). This evaluation can be performed either by manual distribution in paper-based during medical education programs held by clinical departments to gain better responses. But before that, a memo that is written and signed by the hospital director should be endorsed to all departments informing the purposes, significance, and implications of this survey.
- When using paper-based surveys, the acquired responses must be entered into SPSS software after data collection is completed.
- Import the Excel file of a dataset into SPSS software and check for outliers, unengaged responses, and normality. Fix those problems accurately and save it into CSV format.
- Import the converted dataset into SmartPLS software and start the algorithm and bootstrap routine procedures.
- Observe the final results report for the path coefficients significance. If more than 50% of the estimated hypotheses are negative and not significant, execute IPMA for target constructs. If all the effects are significant and positive, perform IPMA as well, observe the endogenous constructs with high performance, and improve the constructs' scores by their indicators. On the contrary, for instance with a non-significant relationship; Service Quality -> Effective Use, the HIS implementation team must continually improve their quick assistance to the users when they are facing problems with the system or computers especially through online or telephone helpdesk supports. Nevertheless, if the total effects score is similar to other indicators within its measured construct, please refer to the lowest performance score between these indicators and take immediate improvement.

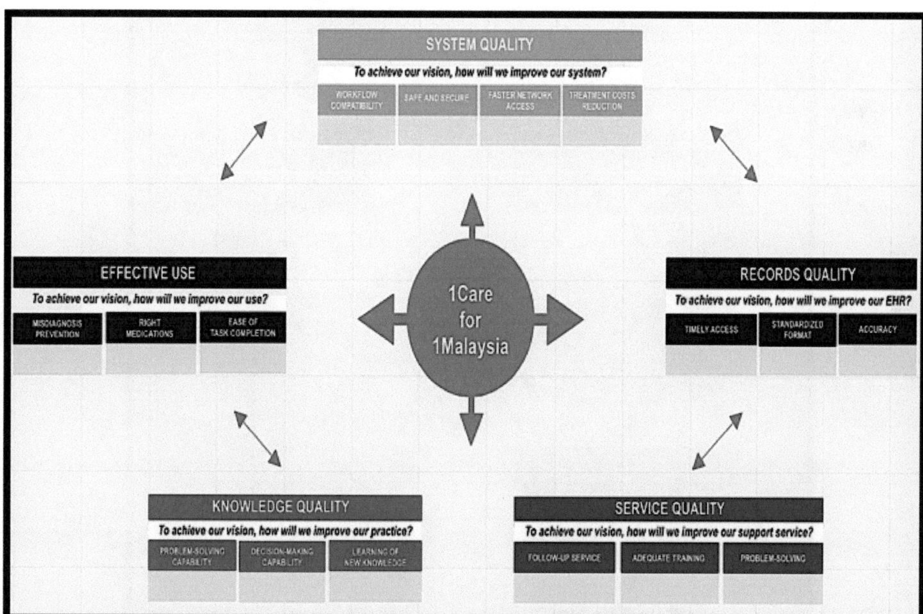

Figure 5. HIS scorecard.

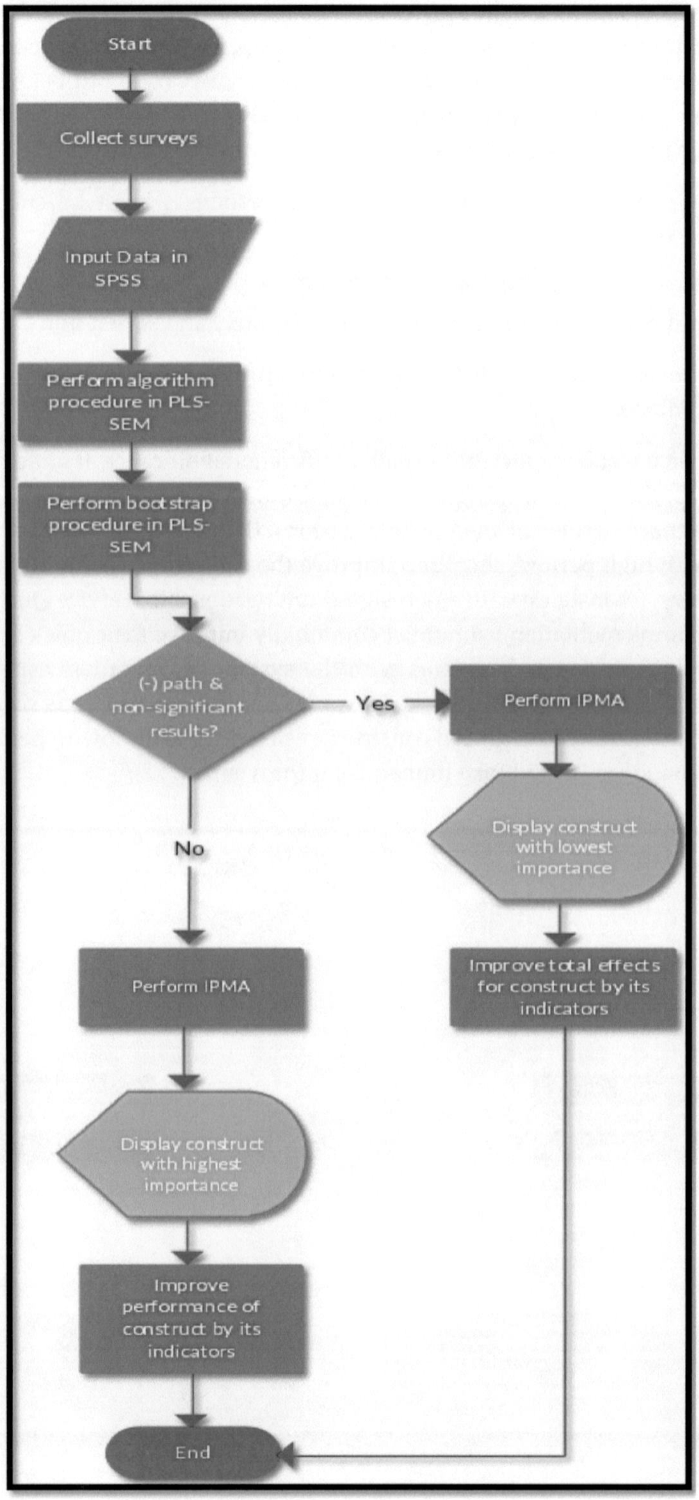

Figure 6. Easy guide to efficiently evaluate your HIS.

http://dx.doi.org/10.5772/68122

Hence, "Easy Guide to Efficiently Evaluate Your HIS" can allow a hospital to assess the system effectiveness efficiently not only at the individual but also at the organizational level by responsible IT department in cooperation with clinical research centers' staffs. Through applying this clear guideline, the precision of HIS performance measurement will be greater and contributes to the effectiveness of the subsequent decision-making by HIS users, stakeholders, and policymakers resulting from a good reputation of successful implementation while reducing costs for future upgrades and sustaining effective use and user performance. The guideline can be the best practical evaluation tool at very minimal cost to be executed for a comprehensive HIS evaluation survey at the national level.

5. Conclusions

The chapter endeavors to identify areas of HIS adoption in which focused effort would yield the most benefit in terms of effective use and user performance. In addressing the present gaps, the study did this by surveying system users at three Malaysian government hospitals using three different HIS packages during postimplementation. When the significance score did not clearly propose which construct and indicators required for operational improvement, the results were extended to include IPMA in ranking the possible constructs and attributes by highlighting the most critical areas for specific responses [58]. As a result, system quality should be maintained for continued effective use and knowledge quality for enhanced user performance. Specifically, effective use must be sustained by improving the design of HISs to fit with clinicians' workflows. Then, the uses of CDSS and CPOE have to be regularly updated with latest features in accelerating patient care with right diagnosis and medications, thus guaranteeing that user performance does not decline. These additional findings also recommend an urgent action by the hospitals relating to the lack of security control and insufficient available computers.

For managerial implications, the extended findings are useful for decision-makers at the government level in allocating proper budgets during strategic planning with HIS scorecard tool for further system upgrades and new implementation at other health facilities. "Easy Guide to Efficiently Evaluate Your HIS" can be a standardized guideline in performing the system effectiveness evaluation survey among IT hospitals. As the performance scores of measuring attributes for all systems did not reach below 50%, the surveyed hospitals must promote the benefits of interoperable systems across the setting, as user performance will be increased exponentially. With high performance but low-importance constructs, it will produce relevant prescriptions for courses of action that the IT departments and system vendors can re-look and immediately fix these issues to avert user dissatisfaction and low productivity. Finally, the hospitals can focus on selected quality criteria and their measuring indicators for these purposes so that more spending may be concentrated on upgrading other health facilities for patient care.

To the best of our knowledge, this study is the first summative evaluation of a country's HISs by utilizing IPMA in the clinical setting. To produce a complete HIS evaluation before and after implementation, it is highly recommended for future health informatics researchers to include IPMA [18] along with new predictor of knowledge quality and improved effective use measures. This technique will therefore increase the rates of health worker's engagement in HIS evaluation survey by indirectly forcing them to choose what they believe to be the most important attributes for the system effectiveness and to rank those attributes by importance score in a clearly map representation. This powerful technique can be extrapolated and applied to other organizations or countries with extreme budget tight while offering efficient resource consumption. In achieving minimal health expenditure, IPMA can be further explored on how it will achieve potential cost savings by prioritizing health-care spending in both developed and developing nations.

Acknowledgements

The authors would like to thank the Director of Health Malaysia for the permission to publish this book chapter. Special appreciation goes to Kedah, Pahang, and Johor Hospitals for their participation in this research. The study received no funding support.

Appendix A: survey questionnaire

1. effuse_1: HIS enables me to complete my tasks successfully in a few easy steps.
2. effuse_2: HIS allows me to prevent misdiagnosis.
3. effuse_3: HIS allows me to provide the right medications to patients.
4. adin_1: Faster network access is critical for me to use HIS.
5. adin_2: Adequate computer hardware is critical for me to use HIS.
6. sysi_1: I only need to enter and save data once, then use the system with multiple HIS modules.
7. sysi_2: The cost for patient's treatment is reduced with the use of HIS.
8. sysi_3: The connection between different HISs is critical to enable coordinated patient care.
9. secc_1: I believe my HIS does not allow unauthorized access.
10. secc_2: I believe my HIS protects patient's information.
11. secc_3: I believe my HIS has a robust security control.
12. secc_4: I feel secure and safe using HIS.
13. syscom_1: HIS fits my workflows.
14. syscom_2: HIS fits the way I work and my work styles.
15. syscom_3: HIS fits my clinical practices.
16. syscom_4: HIS fits my patients' needs.
17. recqual_1: Access to HIS contents is timely.
18. recqual_2: HIS contents are consistent when viewing from other computers.

19. recqual_3: HIS contents are available in a standardized format.

20. recqual_4: HIS contents are accurate.

21. recqual_5: HIS contents avoid duplication of diagnostic tests.

22. recqual_6: HIS contents are complete.

23. servqual_1: IT support staff/vendor provides quick assistance when I face problems with HIS.

24. servqual_2: IT support staff/vendor is always able to solve my problems with HIS.

25. servqual_3: IT support staff/vendor provides follow-up service to HIS users like me.

26. servqual_4: IT support staff/vendor provides adequate training for me to use HIS.

27. knowqual_1: HIS is useful for learning new medical knowledge.

28. knowqual_2: HIS is useful when researching or creating new medical knowledge.

29. knowqual_3: HIS is helpful when applying medical knowledge to my tasks.

30. knowqual_4: HIS helps me share my medical knowledge with others.

31. knowqual_5: HIS provides knowledge that increases my ability to make clinical decisions.

32. knowqual_6: HIS provides knowledge that improves my ability to solve clinical problems.

33. knowqual_7: HIS provides a complete medical source that I can refer to for more information.

34. hcperf_1: HIS increases my time with patients.

35. hcperf_2: HIS enhances the safety of patient care.

36. hcperf_3: HIS increases my work productivity.

37. hcperf_4: HIS increases my chance of obtaining better annual performance marks.

Author details

Mohd Idzwan Mohd Salleh[1,2]*, Rosni Abdullah[1,3] and Nasriah Zakaria[1,4]

*Address all correspondence to: mdidzwan83@gmail.com

1 School of Computer Sciences, Universiti Sains Malaysia, Penang, Malaysia

2 Faculty of Information Management, Universiti Teknologi MARA Malaysia, Kelantan, Malaysia

3 National Advanced IPv6 Centre of Excellence, Universiti Sains Malaysia, Penang, Malaysia

4 Medical Informatics and e-Learning Unit, Medical Education Department, College of Medicine, King Saud University, Saudi Arabia

References

[1] Gheorghiu B, Hagens S. Measuring interoperable EHR adoption and maturity: A Canadian example. BMC Medical Informatics and Decision Making [Internet]. 2016;16(1):1-7. Available from: http://dx.doi.org/10.1186/s12911-016-0247-x.

[2] Strudwick G, Booth R, Mistry K. Can social cognitive theories help us understand nurses' use of electronic health records?. CIN: Computers, Informatics, Nursing [Internet]. 2016 [cited 2016 Feb 16];34(4):169-74. Available from: http://europepmc.org/abstract/med/26844529.

[3] Wen K, Kreps G, Zhu F, Miller S. Consumers' perceptions about and use of the Internet for personal health records and health information exchange: analysis of the 2007 Health Information. Journal of medical Internet research [Internet]. 2010 [cited 2016 Feb 16]; Available from: http://www.jmir.org/2010/4/e73/?trendmd-shared=1.

[4] Lammers E, Adler-Milstein J, Kocher K. Does health information exchange reduce redundant imaging? Evidence from emergency departments. Medical care [Internet]. 2014 [cited 2016 Feb 16]; Available from: http://journals.lww.com/lww-medicalcare/Abstract/2014/03000/Does_Health_Information_Exchange_Reduce_Redundant.7.aspx.

[5] Jensen LGL, Bossen C. Factors affecting physicians' use of a dedicated overview interface in an electronic health record: The importance of standard information and standard. International Journal of Medical Informatics [Internet]. 2016 [cited 2016 Apr 5];87:44-53. Available from: http://www.sciencedirect.com/science/article/pii/S1386505615300769.

[6] Häyrinen K, Saranto K, Nykänen P. Definition, structure, content, use and impacts of electronic health records: A review of the research literature. International Journal of Medical Informatics [Internet]. 2008 May [cited 2014 Jul 10];77(5):291-304. Available from: http://www.ncbi.nlm.nih.gov/pubmed/17951106.

[7] Ghazisaeedi M, Mohammadzadeh N, Safdari R. Electronic health record (EHR) as a vehicle for successful health care best practice. Medical Archives [Internet]. 2014 [cited 2016 Feb 25];68(6):419. Available from: http://www.scopemed.org/?mno=175185.

[8] El-Kareh R, Hasan O, Schiff GD. Use of health information technology to reduce diagnostic errors. BMJ Quality & Safety [Internet]. 2013 Jul;22 Suppl 2(August):ii40–ii51. Available from: http://www.ncbi.nlm.nih.gov/pubmed/23852973%5Cnhttp://qualitysafety.bmj.com/content/22/Suppl_2/ii40.full.pdf.

[9] Reis S, Sagi D, Eisenberg O, Kuchnir Y. The impact of residents' training in Electronic Medical Record (EMR) use on their competence: report of a pragmatic trial. Patient education and ... [Internet]. 2013 [cited 2016 Jan 29]; Available from: http://www.sciencedirect.com/science/article/pii/S0738399113003145.

[10] Dhumal P. Financial model for investment recovery period in electronic health records implementations. International Journal of Economics and Business Research [Internet]. 2014 [cited 2016 Jan 30];9(1):65-79. Available from: http://www.inderscienceonline.com/doi/abs/10.1504/IJEBR.2015.066015.

[11] Gagnon MP, Ghandour EK, Talla PK, Simonyan D, Godin G, Labrecque M, et al. Electronic health record acceptance by physicians: Testing an integrated theoretical model. Journal of Biomedical Informatics [Internet]. Academic Press Inc.; 2014 Apr [cited 2014 Oct 2];48:17-27. Available from: http://www.ncbi.nlm.nih.gov/pubmed/24184678.

[12] Salleh MIM, Abdullah R, Zakaria N. Validating electronic health records system effectiveness questionnaire using partial least squares-structural equation modeling. Australian Journal of Basic and Applied Sciences [Internet]. 2015;9(25):87-95. Available from: http://www.ajbasweb.com/old/ajbas/2015/Special IPN Langkawi (Aug)/87-95.pdf.

[13] Hassan R, Tajuddin MZM. Implementation of total hospital information system (THIS) in Malaysian public hospitals: Challenges and future prospects. International Journal of Business and Social Research [Internet]. 2012 [cited 2016 Feb 24];2:33-41. Available from: http://thejournalofbusiness.org/index.php/site/article/view/189.

[14] Bahagian Perancangan dan Pembangunan KKM. Laporan Kajian Separuh Penggal, Pelan Strategik KKM 2011-2015. Putrajaya; 2014.

[15] Bahagian Perancangan dan Pembangunan KKM. Country Health Plan 10th Malaysia Plan 2011-2015. Putrajaya; 2011.

[16] Lee HW, Ramayah T, Zakaria N. External factors in hospital information system (HIS) adoption model: A case on Malaysia. Journal of Medical Systems [Internet]. 2012 [cited 2016 Feb 24];36(4):2129-40. Available from: http://link.springer.com/article/10.1007/s10916-011-9675-4.

[17] Khalifa M. Organizational, financial and regulatory challenges of implementing hospital information systems in Saudi Arabia. Journal of Health Informatics in Developing Countries. 2016;10(1):30-45.

[18] Cohen JF, Coleman E, Kangethe MJ. An importance-performance analysis of hospital information system attributes: A nurses' perspective. International Journal of Medical Informatics [Internet]. Elsevier Ireland Ltd; 2015;86:82-90. Available from: http://www.sciencedirect.com/science/article/pii/S1386505615300526.

[19] Salleh MIM, Zakaria N, Abdullah R. The influence of system quality characteristics on health care providers' performance: Empirical evidence from Malaysia. Journal of Infection and Public Health [Internet]. King Saud Bin Abdulaziz University for Health Sciences; 2016;(September):1-10. Available from: http://dx.doi.org/10.1016/j.jiph.2016.09.002.

[20] Booth RG. Examining the functionality of the DeLone and McLean information system success model as a framework for synthesis in nursing information and communication technology research. CIN: Computers, Informatics, Nursing [Internet]. 2012 [cited 2016 Oct 19];30(6):330-45. Available from: http://journals.lww.com/cinjournal/Abstract/2012/06000/Examining_the_Functionality_of_the_DeLone_and.9.aspx.

[21] Holden RJ, Karsh BT. The technology acceptance model: Its past and its future in health care. Journal of Biomedical Informatics [Internet]. 2010 [cited 2016 Apr 2];43(1):159-72. Available from: http://www.sciencedirect.com/science/article/pii/S1532046409000963.

[22] Nguyen L, Bellucci E, Nguyen LT. Electronic health records implementation: An evaluation of information system impact and contingency factors. International Journal of Medical Informatics [Internet]. Elsevier Ireland Ltd; 2014 Jul 22 [cited 2014 Sep 8];83(11):779-96. Available from: http://www.ncbi.nlm.nih.gov/pubmed/25085286.

[23] Bossen C, Jensen LG, Udsen FW. Evaluation of a comprehensive EHR based on the DeLone and McLean model for IS success: Approach, results, and success factors. International Journal of Medical Informatics [Internet]. Elsevier Ireland Ltd; 2013 [cited 2016 Feb 24];82(10):940-53. Available from: http://www.sciencedirect.com/science/article/pii/S1386505613001287.

[24] DeLone W, McLean E. Information systems success: The quest for the dependent variable. Information Systems Research [Internet]. 1992 [cited 2015 Jul 23];3(1):60-95. Available from: http://pubsonline.informs.org/doi/abs/10.1287/isre.3.1.60.

[25] DeLone WH, McLean ER. Information systems success revisited. Proceedings of the 35th Annual Hawaii International Conference on System Sciences [Internet]. 2002. p. 2966-76. Available from: http://ieeexplore.ieee.org/lpdocs/epic03/wrapper.htm?arnumber=994345.

[26] Yusof MM, Paul RJ, Stergioulas LK. Towards a framework for health information systems evaluation. Proceedings of the 39th Annual Hawaii International Conference on System Sciences. IEEE; 2006. p. 1-10.

[27] Li F. A framework for examining relationships among electronic health record (EHR) system design, implementation, physicians' work impact [Internet]. University of Southern California; 2014 [cited 2015 Apr 26]. Available from: http://gradworks.umi.com/36/28/3628222.html.

[28] Abdullah ZS. Hospital information systems implementation framework: Critical success factors for Malaysian public hospitals [Internet]. Curtin University; 2013 [cited 2015 Apr 26]. Available from: http://espace.library.curtin.edu.au/cgi-bin/espace.pdf?file=/2013/09/20/file_1/192723.

[29] McGill T, Hobbs V, Klobas J. User developed applications and information systems success: A test of DeLone and McLean's model. Information Resources Management Journal [Internet]. 2003 [cited 2016 Feb 24];16(1):24-45. Available from: http://www.igi-global.com/article/information-resources-management-journal-irmj/1235.

[30] Negash S, Ryan T, Igbaria M. Quality and effectiveness in web-based customer support systems. Information & Management [Internet]. 2003 [cited 2016 Feb 24];40(8):757-68. Available from: http://www.sciencedirect.com/science/article/pii/S0378720602001015.

[31] Sedera D, Tan F. User satisfaction: An overarching measure of enterprise system success. Pacific Asia Conference on Information Systems [Internet]. Bangkok, Thailand; 2005 [cited 2016 Feb 24]. p. 963-76. Available from: http://eprints.qut.edu.au/17079/.

[32] Sedera D, Gable G. A factor and structural equation analysis of the enterprise systems success measurement model. Twenty-Fifth International Conference on Information Systems Proceedings [Internet]. 2004 [cited 2016 Feb 24]. p. 449-64. Available from: http://aisel.aisnet.org/cgi/viewcontent.cgi?article=1124&context=icis2004.

[33] Chang C-S, Chen S-Y, Lan Y-T. Motivating medical information system performance by system quality, service quality, and job satisfaction for evidence-based practice. BMC Medical Informatics and Decision Making [Internet]. 2012 [cited 2015 Jul 23];12(1):1-12. Available from: http://www.biomedcentral.com/1472-6947/12/135?utm_source=twitterfeed&utm_medium=twitter.

[34] Yusof MM, Kuljis J, Papazafeiropoulou, A. Stergioulas LK. An evaluation framework for health information systems: Human, organization and technology-fit factors (HOT-fit). International Journal of Medical Informatics [Internet]. 2008 [cited 2016 Mar 9];77(6):386-98. Available from: http://www.sciencedirect.com/science/article/pii/S1386505607001608.

[35] Salleh MIM, Abdullah R, Zakaria N. Electronic health records' system characteristics, use, and effectiveness: A proposed theoretical framework. In: Soliman KS, editor. Proceedings of The 24th International Business Information Management Association Conference. Milan, Italy: International Business Information Management Association (IBIMA); 2014. p. 1669-81.

[36] Gable GG, Sedera D, Chan T. Re-conceptualizing information system success: The IS-impact measurement model. Journal of the Association for Information Systems [Internet]. 2008 [cited 2016 Feb 24];9(7):377-408. Available from: http://search.proquest.com/openview/5aea21bcb44768af52392e119307e085/1?pq-origsite=gscholar.

[37] Kimiafar K, Sadoughi F, Sheikhtaheri A, Sarbaz M. Prioritizing factors influencing nurses' satisfaction with hospital information systems: A fuzzy analytic hierarchy process approach. CIN: Computers, Informatics, Nursing [Internet]. 2014 [cited 2016 Mar 6];32(4):174-81. Available from: https://www.researchgate.net/profile/Farahnaz_Sadoughi/publication/259956372_Prioritizing_Factors_Influencing_Nurses'_Satisfaction_With_Hospital_Information_Systems_A_Fuzzy_Analytic_Hierarchy_Process_Approach/links/0f3175382a5644c27e000000.pdf.

[38] DeLone WH, McLean ER. The DeLone and McLean model of information systems success: A ten-year update. Journal of Management Information Systems [Internet]. 2003 [cited 2015 Jul 23];19(4):9-30. Available from: http://www.tandfonline.com/doi/abs/10.1080/07421222.2003.11045748.

[39] Lin CH, Wei A, Yang H, Pittayachawan S, Vogel D, Wickramasinghe N. Inquiring knowledge management systems—A Chinese medicine perspective. Proceedings of the Annual Hawaii International Conference on System Sciences. Kauai, HI: IEEE; 2015. p. 3682-90.

[40] Lin, C., Yang, W., Pittayachawan, S., & Wickramasinghe N. Using IS/IT to support the delivery of Chinese medicine: The design of a Chinese medicine clinic system. 24th Australasian Conference on Information Systems [Internet]. Melbourne, Australia: RMIT University; 2013 [cited 2016 Apr 6]. p. 1-10. Available from: https://researchbank.rmit.edu.au/view/rmit:22820.

[41] Chang I-C, Li Y-C, Wu T-Y, Yen DC. Electronic medical record quality and its impact on user satisfaction—Healthcare providers' point of view. Government Information

Quarterly [Internet]. Elsevier Inc.; 2012 Apr [cited 2014 Sep 22];29(2):235-42. Available from: http://linkinghub.elsevier.com/retrieve/pii/S0740624X12000068.

[42] Aldekhail MS. Effect of knowledge management based error mitigation techniques in medical and diagnostic applications. International Conference on Convergence and Security (ICITCS). Beijing: IEEE; 2014. p. 1-6.

[43] Bordoloi P, Islam N. Knowledge management practices and healthcare delivery: A contingency framework. Electronic Journal of Knowledge Management. 2012;10(2):110-20.

[44] Tsai J, Hung S. Determinants of knowledge management system adoption in healthcare. Journal of Organizational Computing and Electronic Commerce [Internet]. 2016 [cited 2016 Jun 16];2-58. Available from: http://www.tandfonline.com/doi/abs/10.1080/10919392.2016.1194062.

[45] Huang YH, Gramopadhye AK. Recommendations for health information technology implementation in rural hospitals. International Journal of Health Care Quality Assurance. 2016;29(4):1-22.

[46] Gray C. Electronic health record systems in a centralized computing services environment: Critical success factors for implementation [Internet]. Robert Morris University; 2014 [cited 2015 Jul 23]. Available from: http://gradworks.umi.com/36/28/3628910.html.

[47] Mansoor MME, Majeed R. Achieving interoperability among healthcare organizations [Internet]. Blekinge Institute of Technology; 2010 [cited 2015 Jul 23]. Available from: http://www.diva-portal.org/smash/record.jsf?pid=diva2:831672.

[48] Yousafzai S, Pallister J, Foxall G. Multi-dimensional role of trust in Internet banking adoption. The Service Industries Journal [Internet]. 2009 May [cited 2014 Oct 22];29(5):591-605. Available from: http://www.tandfonline.com/doi/abs/10.1080/02642060902719958.

[49] Tulu B, Burkhard R, Horan T. Information systems and health care xiv: Continuing use of medical information systems by medical professionals: Empirical evaluation of a work system model. Communications of the Association for Information Systems [Internet]. 2006 [cited 2015 Jul 23];18(1):641-56. Available from: http://aisel.aisnet.org/cgi/viewcontent.cgi?article=3102&context=cais.

[50] Wu J-HJ, Wang Y-MY. Measuring KMS success: A respecification of the DeLone and McLean's model. Information & Management [Internet]. 2006 Sep [cited 2014 Jul 28];43(6): 728-39. Available from: http://linkinghub.elsevier.com/retrieve/pii/S0378720606000498.

[51] Hair JF, Hult GTM, Ringle C, Sarstedt M. A primer on partial least squares structural equation modeling (PLS-SEM) [Internet]. Thousand Oaks, CA: SAGE; 2014 [cited 2015 Aug 19]. 328 p. Available from: https://books.google.com/books?hl=en&lr=&id=TjzABAAAQBAJ&oi=fnd&pg=PR1&dq=A+primer+on+partial+least+squares+structural+equation+modeling+(PLS-SEM)&ots=hy2q9NQfnG&sig=SOp8hQyxw7Mk9cX1wtt92-PXZNY.

[52] Hair JF, Ringle CM, Sarstedt M. PLS-SEM: Indeed a silver bullet. The Journal of Marketing Theory and Practice [Internet]. 2011 [cited 2015 Aug 17];19(2):139-52. Available from: http://www.tandfonline.com/doi/abs/10.2753/MTP1069-6679190202.

[53] Fornell C, Larcker DF. Evaluating structural equation models with unobservable variables and measurement error. Journal of Marketing Research [Internet]. 1981 [cited 2015 Jul 23];18:39-50. Available from: http://www.jstor.org/stable/3151312.

[54] Chin WW. How to write up and report PLS analyses. Handbook of Partial Least Squares [Internet]. Springer Berlin Heidelberg; 2010 [cited 2015 Jul 23]. p. 655-90. Available from: http://link.springer.com/chapter/10.1007/978-3-540-32827-8_29.

[55] Hair JF, Hult GTM, Ringle CM, Sarstedt M. A primer on partial least squares structural equation modeling (PLS-SEM). 2nd ed. Thousand Oaks, CA: SAGE; 2017. 361 p.

[56] Hock C, Ringle CM, Sarstedt M. Management of multi-purpose stadiums: Importance and performance measurement of service interfaces. International Journal of Services Technology and Management. 2010;14(2-3):188-207.

[57] Gustafsson A, Johnson MD. Determining attribute importance in a service satisfaction model. Journal of Service Research [Internet]. 2004 [cited 2016 Nov 3];7(2):124-41. Available from: http://jsr.sagepub.com/content/7/2/124.short.

[58] Ringle CM, Sarstedt M. Gain more insight from your PLS-SEM results: The importance-performance map analysis. Industrial Management & Data Systems. 2016;116(9): 1865-86.

[59] Abalo J, Varela J, Manzano V. Importance values for importance-performance analysis: A formula for spreading out values derived from preference rankings. Journal of Business Research. 2007;60(2):115-21.

[60] Sethna BN. Extensions and testing of importance-performance analysis. Business Economics [Internet]. 1982 [cited 2016 Nov 3];28-31. Available from: http://www.jstor.org/stable/23482618.

Chapter 4

European Health System Typologies: Last 30 Years Under Review

Aida Isabel Pereira Tavares

Additional information is available at the end of the chapter

http://dx.doi.org/10.5772/67536

Abstract

The quest of the researcher to classify national health systems into homogeneous groups has a long history. In this paper, the last 30 years are divided in two periods (1985–2000 and 2000–2015) in order to present and briefly describe the most influential national health system typologies.

Keywords: health systems, Europe, typologies, historical perspective

1. Introduction

European countries display diversified arrangements to provide health care, to finance, and to cover health insurance expenditures. These organized arrangements constitute the health system of each country.

The definition of health system has evolved over time since Alma Ata Declaration in 1978 [1]. Several definitions have been proposed, either by single authors (such as Weinerman [2] and Long [3]) or by institutions (such as the World Bank [4] and WHO [5]).

The most widely accepted definition was published in 2007 in the report "Everybody's business: strengthening health systems to improve health outcomes: WHO's framework for action, 2007" [6]. The definition of health system here is given as "a system of all organizations, people and actions whose primary intentions are to promote, restore or maintain health," which includes efforts to influence determinants of health, as well as more direct health-improving activities.

The WHO definition implicitly considers the goals of a (national) health system. These goals are both final and intermediate [7]. The final goals of a health system are responsiveness to people's expectations, social and financial risk and fair protection, and improved health; the intermediate goals on their turn are improving access, improving coverage, delivering high quality and safe health services, promoting healthy behavior, and improving efficiency.

These goals justify the functions of health systems themselves. The WHO [5] proposes four functions of a health system which are (i) health service provision, (ii) health generation of resources (investment and training), (iii) stewardship, and (iv) health financing (collecting, pooling, and purchasing). The functions of the health systems may be described as follows:

(i) The *provision* (*also referred as delivery*) of health-care services which requires the management of resources and the creation of human resources, delivery of medications, medical services, and medical equipment.

(ii) The *generation of resources* which implies not only their management, but also their creation. While some inputs may be gathered in short term after the investment, other resources may take a long time to obtain and train as the human resources.

(iii) *Stewardship* or overall system oversight which sets the context and policy framework for the overall health system. This function is usually (but not always) a governmental responsibility, where the health priorities, the institutional framework, the activities that should be coordinated with other systems, and the information needed to support the decision-making process are set.

(iv) *Financing or funding* which includes collecting revenues, pooling financial risk, and allocating revenue. (a) The collection of revenue may be done in different ways, and it includes general taxation, donor financing, mandatory payroll contributions, mandatory or voluntary risk-rated contributions (premiums), direct household out-of-pocket expenditures, and other forms of personal savings. (b) Risk pooling refers to the management of financial resources in order to spread the risk from an individual to the pool of individuals, reducing in this way the overall risk for the system. (c) Strategic purchasing or financing of the supply side means the way providers and purchasers establish an interaction and develop service delivery models.

The functions of the health system have been used as dimensions or criteria of classification of health systems. Most traditional criteria used are proxies of financing and delivery functions. But other criteria have been used to capture features of resource generation and stewardship, such as health system actors, cost-sharing, medical technology, and decentralization. Several typologies have been proposed in the last 30 years; some are simple and based on a single criterion, and others are more complex and based on statistical analysis.

The aim of this work is to review the most influential typologies created in the last 30 years to classify the European health systems. The different typologies are summarized, and their most significant features are presented. The contribution of this article is mainly of twofold. On the one hand, it provides a synthesized historical review of how national health systems have been studied over time in Europe; on the other hand, it allows for the possibility to easily describe, criticize, and analyze the evolution of a single health system in the last 30 years.

http://dx.doi.org/10.5772/67536

Additionally, the implicit purpose of this work is to provide an informative and friendly view on how different authors have positioned European health systems in a criteria line or matrix. Some other works in the literature may devote some paragraphs to this theme, but no work is exclusively dedicated to the historical review of health system typologies. These typologies, which are considered as the most influential, were found after a literature review and scholar Google search based on the terms "health system classification"/"health system typologies."

2. Why classify health systems?

The classification of national health systems in groups which share identical characteristics according to some predefine criteria has been of interest of researchers and policy makers. The purposes for the produced typologies are several. Firstly, classification is a step on the process of cognition and knowledge, and it also provides order in a world of infinite instances [8]. Secondly, it allows the international comparison of different national health systems, mainly in terms of their functions. Actually, the nature of classifying health systems is itself a reply to the conceptual need of labeling the different nature of health systems. Thirdly, clustering national health systems allows the assessment of their performance, across countries and time, measured by the attained goals. But also policy assessment and policy recommendation are possible uses from typologies by studying the best references or cases in each group [9]. Finally, a last potential contribution from the typologies of health systems is the historical and comparative analysis that may be developed.

The creation of typologies of health systems can result from a deductive or an inductive method of research [8]. In this work, typologies presented have a deductive nature because it covers more European countries. The inductive method is usually centered in few cases which are presented as examples.

The research to create typologies continues nowadays and so the debate about which dimensions and variables are to be considered, whether or not national health systems fall into defined groups, and which countries may best represent a particular type [8]. Despite this debate, researchers agree on one issue. There is no pure health system in Europe where health systems tend to be set of mixture characteristics. So, aggregating health systems to create a typology is usually based on the principle of the dominant characteristic(s) or on some proximity measure between different indicators.

3. European health system classifications: a historical perspective

The European health systems have been classified in a variety of ways in the last 30 years. Depending on the author, on the purpose, on the criteria, and on the moment, a typology is created. In this work, the last 30 years are divided into two periods, before and after the 2000s. In the more recent period, different proposals are grouped according to the method used to classify health-care systems. The methods used to create the typologies may be non-analytical or analytical. The non-analytical is based on descriptive and/or qualitative analysis, while the analytical is sustained in statistical methods, such as principal component analysis and cluster analysis.

The diversity of proposals is relevant and provides value added on the general and analytical perspective about each health system. In **Table 1** of the Appendix, a synthesis of the set of typologies referred here is presented for a clear perspective of the 30 years of European health system classification. This table lists the author (year), type of analysis/methods, classifying criteria, and typology/countries in each typology.

3.1. Period 1985–2000

In the period 1985–2000, there are four well-known typologies in the literature: three of them are constructed using the unique criterion of funding, and the fourth typology and oldest is based on the three criteria of classification: coverage, funding, and ownership. There is a fifth typology worth to be referred, for curiosity, which is based on geographical neighborhood.

(1) Let us start from the oldest typology from these 30 years. This typology was proposed by OECD [10], in 1987, in a work supervised of George J. Schieber. Using the three criteria reflecting health system functions, health systems are classified into three types: *Beveridge model, Bismarck model,* and private insurance. This last type of health system could not be found in Europe. This typology was very well received, and it has been referred ever since. *Beveridge model* is defined by universal coverage, taxed funded, and public ownership of provision. The *Bismarck model,* on his turn, is defined by universal coverage, social contributions funded, and provision is done by public or private or both sectors. Despite the importance of this typology, it did not classify all European countries, and it placed some dominance in the criterion of financing.

(2) In another work proposed by the WHO under the direction of Saltmann and Figueras [11] and inspired by the OECD typology, three-group typology is proposed. Based on one criterion of funding, three groups are identified: the *Beveridge model, the Bismarck model,* and the *Mixed model*. The first two groups are identical to those identified before: the *Beveridge model* is mainly financed by taxes, and the *Bismarck model* is based on social insurance. The *Mixed model* gathers health systems which are in transition or in transformation. Systems in transition mean those who have strong features of the *Bismarck model* but are in transition to something

	Regulation	Financing	Provision
National health service	State	State	State
National health insurance	State	State	Private
Social-based mixed system	Societal	Societal	State
Social health insurance	Societal	Societal	Private
Private health-care system	Private	Private	Private
Etatist social health insurance	State	Societal	Private

Table 1. Six types of OECD health-care systems Böhm et al. [22].

else; the systems in transformation account for countries moving from an insurance-based system to a taxed-based system and those moving from a *Semashko system*[1] to an insured-based one (ex-communist countries).

(3) Finally, under the direction of Jakubowski et al., the European Parliament in 1998 [13] has also proposed a typology for classifying national health systems. The criteria of funding continue to be the differentiating factor between groups of countries. But now, the authors have introduced a second layer of funding, the supplementary health system funding. This latter funding accounts for both the direct payments and the private voluntary health insurance payment for supplementary health care. This typology is applied to 15 EU countries, and it reflects the variety of health systems across the European countries.

The typology considers four groups of countries, and their names describe the main features of the health systems in each group: (i) *public taxation/private voluntary health insurance and direct payments;* (ii) *public taxation/direct payments but no private voluntary health insurance;* (iii) *social contributions insurance/private voluntary health insurance, direct payments, and public taxation*; and (iv) *mixed compulsory social insurance and private voluntary health insurance/public taxation, direct payments.*

(4) The last typology presented for this period is proposed by Figueras et al. [14] in 1994 who have used a simple criterion: spatial neighborhood criterion. These authors clustered the national health systems in four groups: *Northern macro-region, Center Western macro-region, Center Eastern macro-region,* and *Southern macro-region.* This typology is clear and simple to apply. Nevertheless, it does not convey information about the type of health systems.

3.2. Period 2000–2015

The period 2000–2015 has brought several new proposals on how to classify health systems due to the increasing interest to compare health system on the international level. The set of typologies presented here is distinguished between the analytical and the non-analytical or descriptive. The latter set of typologies is more descriptive and does not use any statistical analysis to find groups of health systems, while the first set of typologies tends to be more sophisticated in their analysis to determine homogeneous groups.

3.2.1. Non-analytical typologies

(1) The use of the single criterion of funding is still a strategy used to derive groups of national health systems, as it can be found, for instance, in the works by Busse et al. [15] in 2007 and by Thompson et al. [16]. Their proposals are quite similar and countries are grouped identically. Both classify the national health systems in *tax-financed system, social insurance system,* and *mixed model* mainly privately financed. The difference is that Busse et al. differentiate the health systems with high of public share of financing from those with high private share.

[1]The Semashko system [12] was born in the former URSS and implemented in the most former socialist countries. Health-care services are basically a total public health-care system, health facilities were owned by the State, and health professionals were paid by the State. The Semashko system provided a universal access to health care, and therefore no one was excluded. But after the collapse of the socialist regimes, the shortage of financial resources led to a higher contribution of patients who are now obliged to pay direct fees to providers.

(2) Blanchette and Tolley [17], in 2001, combine the private or public nature of involvement in financing and delivery functions, resulting in four types of health systems. The authors could only find two groups of health systems in Europe, in particular, the *publicly financed health systems* with *public or private delivery*. But they have analyzed a small set of European countries and left out the more mixed health systems.

(3) The criterion governing production/technology is introduced by Moran [18] in 2000. This criterion captures the way system of innovation is governed within a health system. Medical technology is largely produced by private actors, who also maintain their property rights, but the validation and safeguard of those property rights may be under the public responsibility. The author uses the term "state" as a notion that captures the institutions related with the governance of consumption, provision, and production. The four suggested clusters of health systems are *supply health-care state, entrenched command and state control, corporatist health-care state*, and *insecure command and control state*, which are next summarized.

(i) *Supply health-care state*: funding is done through private insurance, so access is limited; the public control of costs is limited; private hospitals and doctors remain relatively unchecked; and there are no real constraints to medical innovation adoption. This type of health system cannot be found in Europe. (ii) *Entrenched command and state control*: the governance of consumption is mainly public, and access is based on citizenship; there is strong control of resource allocation by the state; the governance of provision of public owned hospitals and of doctors is subject to extensive public control; and there is a moderate constraint to medical innovation. (iii) *Corporatist health-care state*: funding is made through social insurance contributions; the state has a limited control over health-care costs; the same is true for the governance of provision, where private hospitals are prominent and where there are only some constraints on the private interest of doctors; and there are only some constraints on medical innovation. (iv) *Insecure command and control state*: those are systems similar to the entrenched command and state control health-care systems, but there is nearly no control or influence relative to the private interests; and there is a state governance over provision and doctors, but there coexist a strong private sector, where state influence is very limited.

Despite the introduction of a new perspective to classify health systems, the author applies his typology to only six European countries; it would have been interesting to have it extended to more countries.

(4) Based on descriptive analysis of the relations across providers, payers, and users, in particular, the degree to which health-care financing and delivery is publicly controlled or administered. Docteur and Oxley [19] propose three types of health-care systems, in 2003: *public-integrated model, public-contract model*, and *private insurance/provider model*.

The *public-integrated model* combines on-budget financing of health-care provision with hospital providers that are part of the government sector; doctors and other health-care professionals can be either public employees or private contractors to the health-care authority; and complete population coverage is done under a strict budget. In the *public-contract model*, public payers contract with private health-care providers; the payers can be either a state agency or social security funds; often private hospitals and clinics are run on a nonprofit basis. A *private insurance/provider model* uses private insurance combined with private (often for profit) providers; insurance can be mandatory or voluntary; and payment methods are usually activity based.

The typology proposed by these authors introduces an additional criterion of the control/administration. It is this criterion that allows characterizing health systems according to the type of relations established between the different parties of the health system. However, the classification is only applied to some European countries, and it follows closely the grouping of countries based on the dominance of the financing criterion.

(5) The most recent proposal on types of European health systems has been suggested by the European Union—Committee of the Regions [20], and it accounts for 27 EU countries, missing out Croatia. The original contribution of this work comes from the criterion used. The authors have used the role of local and regional authorities within health management systems to propose a typology. This typology yields five groups of health systems: decentralized, partially decentralized, operatively decentralized, centralized but structured at territorial level, and centralized. The name of each group describes the level of (de)centralization of the health system. The three criteria used to obtain this classification are (i) health funding by the Local and Regional Authorities (LRA); (ii) power and responsibility by LRA with regard to health-related legislative, planning, and implementation functions; and (iii) ownership and management of health-care facilities by LRA.

(6) A team of three researchers, Wendt et al. [21], in 2009 pursued the idea of building a typology based on the three criteria, financing, provision/delivery, and regulation/governance, according to the responsible actor—state/public, non-governmental/societal, and market/private. The resulting theoretical classification generates 27 potential health-care systems, but only 10 of them are plausible to find in real world. The empirical analysis was undertaken by Böhm et al. [22], 4 years later, using cluster analysis on 30 OECD countries. The result of that analysis is a set of six types of health-care systems described in **Table 1**.

3.2.2. *Analytical typologies*

Three typologies next presented share the analytical methodology. In fact, all three use cluster analysis to find out how the different health systems could form homogeneous groups. This form of creating a typology may be less intuitive, but it allows the description on the health system based on common traits sustained by the similarity of statistical information.

(1) In 2009, Wendt [23] used cluster analysis applied to ten health indicators to capture the classifying criteria of financing, provision, institutional characteristics, and health expenditures. The result of this analysis is the three types of health systems: *health service provision oriented*, *universal coverage-controlled access*, and *low-budget restricted access*, next described.

(i) The *health service provision oriented* is described by high level of total health expenditure, high share of public funding, and moderate private out-of-pocket funding; moderate level of inpatient and high level of outpatient healthcare; also by high level of autonomy of self-employed doctors; and high freedom of choice for patients.

(ii) Countries in the *universal coverage-controlled access* group have high share of public health funding, medium level of total health expenditure, moderate level of inpatient, and low level of outpatient healthcare; the access to doctors is highly regulated, and doctors face strict regulation regarding their income arrangement.

(iii) The *low-budget restricted access* health systems are characterized by low level of total health expenditure which is related to the weaker economic position of these countries, high private out-of-pocket payments, high control of patients' access to medical doctors, low level of inpatient, and moderate level of outpatient healthcare; GPs receive in general a fixed salary, and income is strongly regulated and controlled.

(2) In the following year, another analytical typology is proposed by Reibling [24] who introduced new criteria for grouping national health systems. In particular, this author considered gatekeeping, cost-sharing, provider density (GPs, specialists, and nurses), and medical technology (magnetic resonance imaging units/MRI and computed tomography scanners/CT) as dimensions of classification. This author has based his proposal in cluster analysis over eighteen indicators and ended up finding four clusters:

(i) *Financial incentives states* that regulate patients' access to medical doctors mainly by cost-sharing, and there is a high availability of GP, nurses, and medical technology; (ii) *strong gatekeeping and low supply states* with no cost-sharing but extensive gatekeeping arrangements for doctor's visits, low numbers of health-care providers, relatively little medical technology, and some regulatory emphasis on provider density and technology; (iii) *weakly regulated and high supply states* with weak gatekeeping and a high supply of health-care providers; (iv) *mixed regulation states* that combine gatekeeping and cost-sharing arrangements, so there is a strong access regulation; physician densities are moderate, and medical technology is highly available.

(3) Finally, Joumard et al. [25] use a set of 22 indicators on institutional features to create a typology of health-care systems. The variables used in this analysis are several, and they may be grouped in those capturing: (i) the reliance on market mechanisms and regulations to steer the demand and supply of health care, (ii) coverage principles to promote equity, and (iii) budget and management approaches to control public spending. The authors perform a cluster analysis and find six groups of health-care systems: Group 1—private provision and private insurance for basic coverage; Group 2—private provision, public insurance for basic coverage, private insurance beyond basic coverage, and some gatekeeping; Group 3—private provision, public insurance for basic coverage, little private insurance beyond basic coverage, and no gatekeeping; Group 4—public provision and public insurance, no gatekeeping, and ample choice of providers; Group 5—public provision and public insurance, gatekeeping, limited choice of providers, and soft budget constraint; Group 6—public provision and public insurance, gatekeeping, ample choice of providers, and strict budget constraint.

4. Conclusion

Classifying national health systems has been a need of researchers to order and study the diversity of the observed reality. In the last 30 years, the European health systems have been classified according to several criteria which generated a set of different typologies. In this article, the most relevant typologies are presented. Six non-analytical typologies are presented. These typologies' main differentiating factor is the number and the type of criteria used to

http://dx.doi.org/10.5772/67536

deduce and describe the group of health systems. More sophisticated typologies are also presented in the period 2000–2015. These are based on statistical analysis and produce groups of countries which share common statistical traits based on how similar health systems are to each other and different from others. Three well-known typologies of this kind are referred.

The majority of typologies proposed and presented here is based on a descriptive and/or qualitative analysis of health systems. While this method is like filling in a line or matrix of criteria, it is more susceptible to criticism, in particular, from each country expert when comparing countries. Moreover, most of these typologies do not cover a wide range of European countries, preventing any potential comparison.

Recently, the increase of data availability and computer capacity to perform statistical analysis has motivated researchers to look for more objective and sophisticated typologies. Cluster analysis has been used to construct and propose three different typologies presented here. This type of statistical method is based on an algorithm aimed at identifying groups of countries that are similar to each other but different from countries in other groups. The key instrument to measure that similarity is the Euclidean distance. The results depend not only on the number and set of countries but also on the characterizing variables considered. For this reason, each typology is internally valid for a period/year, set of countries, and variables considered.

The most used criterion is financing which clearly reflects the central concern placed on this feature. Financing may be seen as a base of the health system functioning and where all the other functions are standing on. From this point of view, there is a consensual view that health systems may be dominantly Beveridgean, Bismarckean, mixed, or private type. While some countries may show some consistency over time, some countries do change their funding process along time. Future research may focus on how and why changes have occurred and what were the effects on the population health of such changes.

The second most used criterion is provision and delivery. Not only, these functions may be proxied and compared easily with data across countries; they also convey information about the functioning of the health system. The delivery/provision of health care is crucial to improve population health results and performance assessment. The ideas behind this function may be differentiated into access, availability, utilization, and coverage of health care. It is likely that future typologies, in particular, when considering similar health systems, will look for variables that may proxy each of these facets of provision.

Finally, it is worth to notice that authors seem pleased to baptize each group of countries in a typology. Except for those typologies based on the criteria of financing, where some agreement exists for the given names, the remaining typologies present different and creative labels for the groups found. This fact reflects the lack of comparability across typologies. Nevertheless, some researchers may found interesting to analyze the typologies for a single country, a long time, since it provides a multiple view of the health system along time.

Acknowledgements

The author acknowledges the fellowship from EURO_HEALTHY project, European Union's Horizon 2020 grant agreement nr: 643398.

Appendix

Typologies of European health systems in the last 30 years.

Author (year)	Type of analysis/methods Classifying criteria	Typology/countries
Period 1985–2000		
OECD p. 24 [10] responsible author GJ Schieber	Non-analytical/descriptive Coverage Financing Ownership	Beveridge model—UK ands Italy Bismarck model—France and Germany Mixed model—the Netherlands Private insurance—US, no European country
WHO, pp. 115–6 [11] responsible authors R. Saltmann and J. Figueras	Non-analytical/descriptive Financing	Mainly taxed based—Denmark, Finland, Iceland, Ireland, Norway, Sweden, and UK Mainly insurance based—Austria, Belgium, France, Germany, Luxembourg, the Netherlands, and Switzerland Mixed system—three subgroups Systems in transition (mainly Bismarckean type)—Israel and Turkey Systems in transformation I (from insured to taxed system)—Greece, Italy, Portugal, and Spain Systems in transformation II (from Semashko to insured system)—ex-communist countries
European Parliament, p. 18 [13] responsible authors E Jakubowski and R. Busse	Non-analytical/descriptive Financing	Main system/supplementary system Public taxation/private VHI and direct payments—Finland, Greece, Ireland, Italy, Sweden, Spain, and UK Public taxation/direct payments—Denmark, and Portugal Social contributions, insurance/private VHI, direct payments, public taxation—Austria, Belgium, France, Germany, and Luxembourg Mixed compulsory social insurance and private voluntary health insurance/public taxation, direct payments—the Netherlands
Figueras et al. [14]	Non-analytical/descriptive Spatial neighborhood	Northern macro-region—Sweden, Norway, Finland, Denmark, UK, and Ireland Center Western macro-region—France, Germany, Austria, the Netherlands, Belgium, and Luxembourg Center Eastern macro-region—Poland, Czech Republic, Slovakia, Hungary, Slovenia, Estonia, and Lithuania Southern macro-region—Italy, Spain, Portugal, and Greece
Period 2000–2015		
Non-analytical typologies		
Busse et al., p. xi [15]	Non-analytical/descriptive Financing Ownership	Tax-financed system High public share—Denmark, Finland, Ireland, Italy, Spain, Norway, Sweden, and UK High private share—Portugal Social security contribution system High public share—Belgium, France, Germany, Luxembourg, and the Netherlands High private share—Austria and Switzerland Mixed model (mainly private financed)—Greece

Author (year)	Type of analysis/methods Classifying criteria	Typology/countries
Thompson et al., p. 29 [16]	Non-analytical/descriptive Financing	Social insurance—Austria, Belgium, Czech Republic, Estonia, France, Germany, Lithuania, Luxembourg, the Netherlands, Poland, Romania, Slovakia, Slovenia, and Bulgaria Taxed financed—Denmark, Finland, Ireland, Italy, Malta, Portugal, Spain, Sweden, and UK Out-of-pocket financed—Cyprus, Greece, and Latvia
Blanchette and Tolley [17]	Non-analytical/descriptive Financing Delivery	Public financing and public delivery—Norway, Sweden, Denmark, and Finland Public financing and private delivery—Germany, France, and UK
Moran [18]	Non-analytical/descriptive Consumption Delivery/provision technology	Entrenched command and state control—Scandinavia and UK Supply state—US and no European country Corporatist state—Germany Insecure command and control state—Greece, Italy, and Portugal
Docteur and Oxley, p.10 [19]	Non-analytical/descriptive Financing Delivery/provision Control/administration	Public-integrated model—Nordic countries, Italy, Greece, and Portugal Public-contract model—Continental European countries and UK Private insurance/provider—Switzerland
European Union [20]	Non-analytical/descriptive LRA funding LRA power and responsibility LRA ownership and management	Decentralized—Austria, Italy, and Spain Partially decentralized Above EU average funding—Denmark, Estonia, Finland, Lithuania, Poland, Sweden, and Hungary Below EU average funding—Belgium, Czech Republic, and Germany Operatively decentralized Below EU average funding—Bulgaria, Latvia, Luxembourg, Romania, Slovakia, and Slovenia Null or low funding—the Netherlands and UK Centralized but structured at the territorial level—France, Greece, and Portugal Centralized—Cyprus, Ireland, Malta
Wendt et al. [21] and Böhm et al. [22]	Non-analytical/descriptive Financing Delivery/provision Regulation	National health service—Denmark, Finland, Norway, Sweden, Portugal, Spain, and UK National health insurance—Ireland and Italy Social-based mixed type—Slovenia Social health insurance—Austria, Germany, Luxembourg, and Switzerland Etatist social health insurance—Belgium, Estonia, France, Czech Republic, Hungary, the Netherlands, Poland, and Slovakia Private health-care system—no European country and US
Analytical typologies		
Wendt [23]	Cluster analysis Ten indicators for health-care expenditures Financing Delivery/provision Institutional characteristics	Health service provision oriented—Austria, Belgium, France, Germany, and Luxembourg Universal coverage-controlled access—Denmark, Great Britain, Sweden, Italy, and Ireland Low-budget restricted access—Portugal, Spain, and Finland (Greece and the Netherlands could not be grouped)

Author (year)	Type of analysis/methods Classifying criteria	Typology/countries
Reibling [24]	Cluster analysis Eighteen indicators for gatekeeping, cost-sharing provider density, and medical technology	Financial incentives states—Austria, Belgium, France, Sweden, and Switzerland Strong gatekeeping and low-supply states—Denmark, the Netherlands, Poland, Spain, and Great Britain Weakly regulated and high-supply states—Czech Republic, Germany, and Greece Mixed regulation states—Finland, Italy, and Portugal
Joumard et al. [25]	Principal component analysis and cluster analysis Twenty-two indicators for market mechanism coverage/provision financing and management	Group 1: countries relying heavily on market mechanisms—Germany, the Netherlands, Slovakia, and Switzerland Groups 2 and 3: countries with basic insurance coverage and heavy reliance on market mechanisms—Belgium, France/ Austria, Czech Republic, Greece, and Luxembourg Group 4: countries with limited private supply but wide choice of providers—Sweden and Turkey Groups 5 and 6: countries with heavily regulated public systems—Denmark, Finland, Portugal, Spain/Hungary, Ireland, Italy, Norway, Poland, and UK

Author details

Aida Isabel Pereira Tavares

Address all correspondence to: aitavar@gmail.com

CEISUC, Centre of Research in Health of the University of Coimbra, Coimbra, Portugal

References

[1] WHO. Alma Ata Declaration. Available from http://www.who.int/publications/almaata_declaration_en.pdf?ua=1 [accessed: 19/09/2015]; 1978.

[2] Weinerman ER. Research on comparative health service systems. Medical Care. 1971; 9: 272-290.

[3] Long MJ. The Medical Care System: A Conceptual Model. Ann Arbor: AUPHA Press; 1994.

[4] World Bank. World Development Report, Investing in Health. World Developmen Report. New York: Oxford University Press; 1993.

[5] WHO. Healthcare Systems: Improving Performance. World Health Report. Geneve: WHO; 2000.

[6] WHO. Everybody Business: Strengthening Health Systems to Improve Health Outcomes: WHO's Framework for Action. Geneva: WHO; 2007.

[7] WHO. Portugal Health System, Performance Assessment. Copenhagen: WHO Regional Office for Europe; 2010.

[8] Freeman R, Frisina L. Health care systems and the problem of classification. Journal of Comparative Policy Analysis: Research and Practice. 2010; 12(1-2): 163-178. DOI: 10.1080/13876980903076278.

[9] Freeman R. Comparing Health Systems. In Mullner R, editor. Encyclopedia of Health Services Research. Thousand Oak, CA: Sage; 2009.

[10] OECD. Financing and Delivering Healthcare: A Comparative Analysis of OECD Countries. OECD Social Policy Studies. Paris: OECD; 1987.

[11] Saltmann RB, Figueras J. European Health Care Reform. Analysis of Current Strategies, WHO Regional Publications, European Series, No. 72. Copenhagen: WHO Regional Office for Europe; 1997.

[12] Fleck F, Sheiman I. Rock road from the Semashko to a new health model. Bulletin of the World Health Organization. 2013; 91: 320-321.

[13] Jakubowski E, Busse R, Chambers GR. Health Care Systems in the EU. Public Health and Consumer Protection Series SACO 101 EN. Directorate General for Research. Luxembourg: European Parliament; 1998.

[14] Figueras J, Mossialos E, McKee M, and Sassi F. Health care systems in Southern Europe: is there a Mediterranean paradigm?. International Journal of Health Sciences. 1994; 5(4): 135-146.

[15] Busse R, Schreyögg J, Gericke C. Analyzing Changes in Health Financing Arrangements in High-Income Countries: A Comprehensive Framework Approach, Health, Nutrition and Population (HNP) Discussion Paper. Washington, DC. World Bank; 2007.

[16] Thompson S, Foubister T, Mossialos E. Financing Health Care in the European Union, Challenges and Policy Responses. Observatory Studies Series 17. European Observatory on Health Systems and Policies. Copenhagen: WHO Regional Office for Europe; 2009.

[17] Blanchette C and Tolley E. Public and Private Sector Involvement in Health Care Systems: Comparison of OECD Countries. Available from http://publications.gc.ca/Collection-R/LoPBdP/BP/bp438-e.htm [accessed: 19/09/2015]; 2001.

[18] Moran M. Understanding the welfare state: the case of health care. The British Journal of Politics and International Relations. 2000; 2(2): 135-160. DOI: 10.1111/1467-856X.00031.

[19] Docteur E, Oxley H. Health-Care Systems: Lessons From the Reform Experience. OECD Economic Department Working Papers 374 and Health Working Papers 9. Paris: OECD; 2003.

[20] European Union. The Management of Health Systems in the EU Member States—The Role of Local and Regional Authorities. EU Committee of the Regions: Report written by Progress Consulting S.r.l. and Living Prospects Ltd; 2012.

[21] Wendt C., Frisina L. and Rothgang H. (2009) Healthcare System Types: A Conceptual Framework for Comparison. Social Policy & Administration, 43: 70-90. doi:10.1111/j.1467-9515.2008.00647.x

[22] Böhm K, Schmid A, Götze R, Landwehr C, Rothgang H. Five types of OECD healthcare systems: Empirical results of a deductive classification. Health Policy. 2013; 113(3): 258-269. DOI: 10.1016/j.healthpol.2013.09.003.

[23] Wendt C. Mapping European healthcare systems: a comparative analysis of financing, service provision and access to healthcare. Journal of European Social Policy. 2009; 19(5): 432-445. DOI: 10.1177/0958928709344247.

[24] Reibling N. Healthcare systems in Europe: towards an incorporation of patient access. Journal of European Social Policy. 2010; 20(1): 5-18. DOI: 10.1177/0958928709352406.

[25] Joumard I, André C, Nicq C. Health care systems: efficiency and institutions. Economics Department Working Papers 769 (No. ECO/WKP(2010)25). Paris: OECD; 2010.

Chapter 5

Assessment of Avoidable Mortality Concepts in the European Union Countries, Their Benefits and Limitations

Beata Gavurova and Tatiana Vagasova

Additional information is available at the end of the chapter

http://dx.doi.org/10.5772/67818

Abstract

The concept of avoidable mortality is intended to assessing health care system performance. It is defined as premature deaths from selected disease groups that are considered either treatable through the timely and effective health care (amenable mortality), or preventable by public health interventions (preventable mortality). The purpose of study is to analyse the impact of four lists of causes of death created by researchers on amenable mortality by country, sex and cause of death. Data on deaths were obtained from the WHO database for 20 European Union countries in 2014. We applied the method of direct standardisation using the European Standard Population, Spearman rank-order correlation with statistical significance tests and confidence intervals. We found that the selection of diseases considered as amenable has not significantly impact on the cross-country comparison, but the weight of selected list of causes of death is significant at the national level. The concept has several limitations relating to selection of diseases and setting age threshold over time, availability of health care resources, prevalence of diseases or variation of causes of death coding among countries. However, indicator of avoidable mortality offers a way of the evaluating effectiveness of health systems in maintaining and improving population health.

Keywords: avoidable mortality, amenable mortality, preventable mortality, health care system performance, health policy

1. Introduction

Health systems play an important role in improving population health what closely relates to assessing the effectiveness of health care systems as one of the main dimensions of health system performance. Evaluating the effectiveness of health care systems requires pre-defined objectives or the expected health outcomes that are usually measured by mortality and morbidity. More specifically, length of life and quality of life are examined. These aggregate indicators are not able to capture a clear impact of health care activities, especially quality of health care, on the health status of population. Therefore, more specific health outcome indicators were developed, e.g. avoidable mortality by selected causes of death, infant mortality, prevalence or incidence of chronic diseases, avoidable hospitalisations, and others [1].

The question of how much health care contributes to the health of populations has been discussed for several decades. Although there is no indicator that would comprehensively reflect the performance of health care system, nevertheless, the suitable measurement seems to be a concept of avoidable mortality. The concept of avoidable mortality, as an indicator for the quality of health care services, defines premature deaths from selected disease groups that are considered either treatable through the medical services or preventable by influencing the population characteristics [2].

From the beginning 1970s, many researchers have tried to renew the list of causes of death considered as amenable by health care or preventable by health interventions (see Chapter 2). Unfortunately, many studies did not demonstrate the selection process of avoidable causes of death. This is a bias that raises a question if this concept is not influenced by subjective approach of the given researchers. Has this concept a potential to be applied both at national and international levels?

The main objective of this study is to analyse the impact of the four lists of causes of death on amenable mortality by country, sex and cause of death. By application of several methods of avoidable mortality, we have an ambition to point out possible fluctuations in their results and limitations of international comparison. These raise an appeal for confrontation of the scientific teams at national and international levels and for the development of comparative international baseline. The most innovative part of the study is disputation whether the concept of avoidable mortality is reliable for international health systems comparison or not.

This chapter consists of six sections. Theoretical background of avoidable, amenable and preventable mortality, together with a literature review follows Section 1. Section 3 presents the description of the two recent modifications of the concept including cause of death structure. Section 4 deals with the empirical analyses of amenable mortality differentials across the European Union countries and describes the data and methods used. Section 5 provides a discussion about the potentials or limitations of the concept applied. The most meaningful conclusions are summarised at the end of the chapter.

2. Development of the concept of avoidable mortality

The concept of avoidable mortality was developed by Rutstein et al. [3]. They suggested that several diseases at certain ages should not occur in the presence of timely and effective health care. Additionally, they distinguished the diseases that should be amenable by the quality of health care (e.g. diabetes mellitus treated with insulin) and those that were influenced by public health policy interventions (e.g. lung cancer prevented by smoking elimination). Their list of causes of death included more than 90 diseases considered as unnecessary, untimely causes of death and disabilities. Many research studies have tried to renew the list over time adjusting to the new medical and technological advances. In 1983, Charlton et al. [4] modified the number of conditions on 14 disease groups and excluded deaths that were not directly associated with health care, for example, deaths avoided by public health prevention programs comprising alcohol or tobacco consumption. At the end of the 1980s, the concept was proceeded by several researchers [5, 6], but the highest progress was achieved by Holland [7] who created a European Community atlas of avoidable mortality modifying the previous authors. As for a main benefit of the atlas, strict distinguishing between types of health care services on primary care, hospital care and collective health services was interpreted. In 1993 and 1997, second and third editions of atlas adjusting the number of diseases were created by Holland [8, 9] again, and further developed by other authors [10–13]. In spite of changing list of causes of death, age limit was mostly set at 65 years, what was about the average life expectancy in developed countries in those years. According to experts, above this age, the treatment of selected diseases is less obvious and appearance of co-morbidities becomes problematic.

In 2001, Tobias and Jackson [14] derived the weights for primary, secondary and tertiary health interventions on the basis of a medical expert consensus. For example, avoidability of deaths from HIV/AIDS was distributed according to the primary level with weights 0.9, the secondary level with weights 0.05 and the tertiary level weighted 0.05. To compare, deaths from hypertensive disease were avoidable first by secondary interventions with weights 0.65, second by tertiary interventions with weights 0.3 and finally by primary interventions weighted 0.05. Unfortunately, all above-mentioned proposals of the concept of avoidable mortality did not consider the availability of health care resources such as current technology, medical skills, human resources or health expenditures in a certain country.

A new perspective view on the concept was presented by Nolte and McKee [15] in 2004. They conducted a broad review of randomised controlled trials providing the evidence of impact of health services on survival taking into account advances in medical knowledge and technology across the European Union countries during the 1980s and 1990s. The previous lists of causes of death created by Mackenbach et al. [6] or Charlton et al. [4] were changed on 34 groups of diseases comprising amenable, preventable conditions and ischaemic heart disease separately. Ischaemic heart disease was represented as a separate group because the highest number of these deaths could bias the influence of health services on other diseases. Additionally, the concept considers only 50% of deaths from ischaemic heart disease. Another reason was that ischaemic heart disease could be understood partially as amenable but also as preventable cause of death. Some causes of death were added to the list and some were removed. For example, malignant neoplasm of prostate was not included because an available time trends analysis of cancer mortality showed a small decrease of mortality from prostate cancer, together with the uncertain impact of screening. On the other hand, they included colorectal cancer on the basis of randomised controlled trials providing that curative resection had a significant impact on survival. Establishing an upper age limit varied across diseases. The vast majority were set at 75 years, with the exception of diabetes mellitus (lower than 50 years), some infectious and respiratory diseases (lower than 15 years), malignant neoplasm of cervix uteri and body uterus, as well as leukaemia (lower than 45 years). This was the result of studies that reported substantial improvements in mortality from these diseases relating to advances in treatment before mentioned age limits.

The concept was further renewed analysing European and non-European countries due to the works by Nolte and McKee [16] in 2008 and Tobias and Yeh [17] in 2009. Nolte and McKee closely followed up their last list of causes of death from 2004, while Tobias and Yeh discussed some new inclusion and exclusion criteria. Infectious diseases varied significantly. While Nolte and McKee concentrated on infectious disease of children before the age of 15, Tobias and Yeh focused on selective invasive bacterial infections such as scarlet fever, meningococcal infection, etc. They argued that early detection and treatment by antibiotic therapy decrease mortality substantially. Moreover, only half of the mortality from cerebrovascular diseases, ischaemic heart disease and diabetes mellitus are considered as amenable by appropriate health care according to Tobias and Yeh, because the second half can be preventable by health behaviours (e.g. healthy lifestyle, obesity prevention). The authors of mentioned lists of diseases have different opinions on setting age limit for some causes of death; however, there are more similarities than discrepancies between these two lists of diseases (**Table 1**).

Cause of death	Nolte and McKee [16] ICD-10	Tobias and Yeh [17] ICD-10
Infectious disease		
Tuberculosis	A15–A19, B90	A15–A19, B90
Selected invasive infections:		
Intestinal infectious diseases	A00–A09 (age 0–14)	Non-classified
Whooping cough	A37 (age 0–14)	Non-classified
Measles	B05 (age 1–14)	Non-classified
Tetanus and Diphtheria	A35–A36	Non-classified
Sepsis	A40–A41	A40–A41
Scarlet fever	Non-classified	A38
Meningococcal infection	Non-classified	A39
Acute poliomyelitis	A80	Non-classified
Influenza	J10–J11	Non-classified
Pneumonia	J12–J18	J13–J15, J18
Erysipelas	Non-classified	A46
Legionnaires disease	Non-classified	A481
Malaria	Non-classified	B50–B54

http://dx.doi.org/10.5772/67818

Cause of death	Nolte and McKee [16] ICD-10	Tobias and Yeh [17] ICD-10
Meningitis	Non-classified	G00, G03
Cellulitis	Non-classified	L03
Neoplasms		
Colorectal cancer	C18–C21	C18–C21
Malignant neoplasms of skin	C44	C43–C44
Breast cancer	C50	C50
Cervical cancer	C53	C53
Uterine cancer	C54–C55 (age 0–44)	C54–C55
Testis cancer	C62	Non-classified
Bladder cancer	Non-classified	C67
Thyroid cancer	Non-classified	C73
Hodgkin's disease	C81	C81
Leukaemia	C91–C95 (age 0–44)	C91–C95 (age 0–44)
Benign neoplasms	Non-classified	D10–D36
Diabetes mellitus (type 2)	E10–E14 (age 0–49)	E10–E14 (50% of deaths)
Ischaemic heart disease	I20–I25 (50% of deaths)	I20–I25 (50% of deaths)
Other circulatory disease		
Rheumatic and other valvular heart disease	I05–I09	I01–I09
Hypertensive heart disease	I10–I13, I15	I11
Cerebrovascular diseases	I60–I69	I60–I69 (50% of deaths)
Respiratory diseases (excl. pneumonia, influenza) (age 1–14)	J00–J09, J20–J99	Non-classified
Chronic obstructive pulmonary disease	Non-classified	J40–J44 (age >45)
Asthma	Non-classified	J45–J46 (age 0–44)
Surgical conditions		
Peptic ulcer disease	K25–K27	K25–K28
Appendicitis	K35–K38	K35–K38
Hernia	K40–K46	K40–K46
Cholelithiasis, cholecystitis	K80–K81	K80–K83
Pancreatitis	Non-classified	K85–K86
Postcholecystectomy syndrome	Non-classified	K915
Nephritis and nephrosis	N00–N07, N17–N19, N25–N27	I12–I13, N00–N09,N17–N19
Obstructive uropathy and prostatic hyperplasia	N40	N13, N20–N21, N35, N40, N991

Cause of death	Nolte and McKee [16] ICD-10	Tobias and Yeh [17] ICD-10
Misadventures to patients during surgical and medical care	Y60–Y69, Y83–Y84	Non-classified
Maternal, congenital and perinatal conditions		
Maternal deaths	O00–O99	Non-classified
Perinatal deaths, all causes (excl. stillbirths)	P00–P96	H311, P00, P03–P95
Congenital malformations	Q20–Q28	Q00–Q99
Other conditions		
Thyroid disorders	E00–E07	E00–E07
Epilepsy	G40–G41	G40–G41

Note: Age group used for calculation is 0–74 except if otherwise mentioned.
Source: Own processing based on Nolte and McKee [16] and Tobias and Yeh [17].

Table 1. Causes of death selected in the amenable mortality list of Nolte and McKee [16] and Tobias and Yeh [17].

The second latest study 'Amenable mortality in the European Union: toward better indicators for the effectiveness of health systems' (AMIEHS) [18] in 2011 introduced an empirical evidence of selecting diseases into the lists of causes of death. Finally, a recent project has referred to the avoidable mortality indicators defined according to the Eurostat 'Satellite List' Task Force [19] in 2013. A common objective of these studies is to reach a consensus by countries of the European Community about the definition and selection of causes of avoidable deaths. Both studies are further described in Section 3 more specifically for the purposes of our analysis.

3. Conceptual methods

3.1. AMIEHS project from 2011

The AMIEHS project (Amenable mortality in the European Union: toward better indicators for the effectiveness of health systems) was introduced in 2011 by researchers representing prestigious universities from seven EU countries: the Netherland, the United Kingdom, Sweden, France, Estonia, Germany and Spain.

The main aim of this project is to develop an agreed definition of amenable mortality for Europe and introduce a renewed way of selecting diseases into the lists of causes of death that are amenable by health care which can be used in assessing effectiveness of health systems. They applied strict selection process of diseases based on the consecutively conducted analyses. First, they identified 54 diseases for which mortality declined more than 30% between 1979 and 2000, and for which the number of deaths in 2000 exceeded 100 in England or Wales. These countries were selected because they disposed the most consistent data over this period. Second, they conducted a systematic review of the literature in order to identify health care interventions, which were introduced in 1970–2000 and shown as effective in reducing mortality.

Evidence of effectiveness of interventions was evaluated on a four-point scale. The highest grade was denoted as (4)—evidence from systematic reviews or meta-analysis; (3)—randomised controlled trial; (2)—observational studies; and (1)—consensus statements or expert opinions. Grade of evidence of the decrease in mortality of 30% or more due to effective impact of health care interventions was evaluated on a three-point scale: (3)—evidence from population-based registers (e.g. cancer registries) of reduction in mortality; (2)—published studies describing decline in mortality at population level where investigation has identified health care interventions as the most likely explanation; and (1)—published studies describing decline in mortality at population level where investigation has identified health care interventions as one among several explanations.

However, the strength of the evidence was variable, only few interventions had the highest grade and many interventions were supported by evidence from observational studies only. The highest levels of evidence were observed, for example, in HIV-related mortality that between 1996 and 1998 fell by 60% in the United States due to the key intervention attributable to the azidothymidine and zidovudine applied in the late 1980s. Evidence of patient-level studies reflected a major influence of treatment on mortality during the early 1990s. The result of these efforts was the list of 16 causes of death for which a review of the literature indicated the appropriate level of evidence of treatment (**Table 2**). Those causes of death, in which successful health care interventions were introduced before 1970, e.g. infectious diseases treated successfully with antibiotics or diabetes by insulin were eliminated from the list of amenable causes of death.

Cause of death	AMIEHS (2011) ICD-10	EUROSTAT (2013) ICD-10
Infectious disease		
Tuberculosis	Non-classified	A15–A19, B90
Selected invasive bacterial and protozoal infections	Non-classified	A38–A41, A46, A481,B50–B54, G00, G03, J02, L03
Hepatitis C	Non-classified	B171, B182
HIV	B20–B24	B20–B24 (all ages)
Neoplasms		
Colorectal cancer	C18–C21	C18–C21
Malignant neoplasms of skin	Non-classified	C43
Breast cancer	C50	C50
Cervical cancer	C53	C53
Testis cancer	C62	Non-classified
Bladder cancer	Non-classified	C67

Cause of death	AMIEHS (2011) ICD-10	EUROSTAT (2013) ICD-10
Thyroid cancer	Non-classified	C73
Hodgkin's disease	C81	C81
Leukaemia	C91	C91, C920 (age 0–44)
Benign neoplasms	Non-classified	D10–D36
Diabetes mellitus (type 2)	Non-classified	E10–E14 (age 0–49)
Ischaemic heart disease	I20–I25	I20–I25
Other circulatory disease		
Rheumatic and other valvular heart disease	I00–I09	I01–I09
Hypertensive heart disease	I10–I13	I10–I15
Heart failure	I50–I51	Non-classified
Cerebrovascular diseases	I60–I69	I60–I69
Respiratory diseases		
Influenza (including swine flu)	Non-classified	J09–J11
Pneumonia	Non-classified	J12–J18
Asthma	Non-classified	J45–J46
Surgical conditions		
Gastric and duodenal ulcer	K25–K26	K25–K28
Acute abdomen, appendicitis, intestinal obstruction, cholecystitis/lithiasis, pancreatitis, hernia	Non-classified	K35–K38, K40–K46, K80–K83, K85, K861–K869, K915
Nephritis and nephrosis	N17–N19	N00–N07, N17–N19, N25–N27
Obstructive uropathy and prostatic hyperplasia	Non-classified	N13, N20–N21, N35, N40, N991
Congenital and perinatal conditions		
Complications of perinatal period	P00–P96	P00–P96, A33 (all ages)
Congenital malformations, deformations and chromosomal anomalies	Q20–Q24	Q00–99
Other condition		
Epilepsy and status epilepticus	Non-classified	G40–G41
Misadventures to patients during surgical and medical care	Non-classified	Y60–Y69, Y83–Y84 (all ages)

Note: Age group used for calculation is 0–74 except if otherwise mentioned.

Source: Own processing based on AMIEHS and EUROSTAT's proposals.

Table 2. Comparison of the AMIEHS and the EUROSTAT's list of causes of death considered amenable to health care.

For each selected cause of death, mortality trends were analysed using regression analyses to specify points in time at which the mortality trend changed significantly. They applied age limit 75 years of age. The trend analyses examined the validation of amenable mortality indicators. The results were also validated by a Delphi method where experts assessed the likelihood that variations in mortality from the pre-selected conditions reflect variations in the effectiveness of health care. Surprisingly, the experts reached consensus on only three diseases: colorectal cancer, cervical cancer and cerebrovascular disease. These results raise doubts about availability of amenable mortality as a valid indicator of effectiveness of health systems in international comparisons. Their analyses showed that although the treatment for surgical emergencies has been known for decades, mortality has continued to decline, reflecting a combination of some other factors, for example, increasing skill in treatment or better treatment of complications. However, the AMIEHS project has proved that amenable mortality partially reflects the impact of health care innovations but must be interpreted with other analyses examining such as quality of health care utilisation or access to health care resources.

Finally, an electronic atlas of amenable mortality was prepared that provides trends of standardised mortality rates in European countries according to the list of causes of death over the period 2001–2009 [20].

3.2. Eurostat task force on satellite lists of causes of death from 2013

At the request of European member states, policy makers and experts in the field of public health to enhance information on specific groups of causes of death, Eurostat established a Task Force for revising a Satellite Lists of causes of death information on major public health issues. These public health themes also include the two concepts of avoidable mortality: amenable and preventable deaths. This satellite list should serve as a comprehensive information platform on at-risk groups of population in the European countries. The Task Force had some meetings were decided to consider the list of avoidable causes of death based on the three publications by the Office for National Statistics of the United Kingdom.

First of them, the consultation document [21] from February 2011 consists of the literature review, comparative analyses of existing selections of causes and consultations with experts to agree or disagree with the proposed disease classification. A public consultation was running between February and April 2011. The second one was the 'Responses to the public consultation on definitions of avoidable mortality' [22] from August 2011. This document contains 20 responses to the consultation document from various medical experts on five key questions of revising the definition of avoidable mortality concept. These questions related to the proposed causes of death to be included in amenable or preventable mortality, agreement or disagreement with the proposals on age limits, and how they would change them. Third, the final definition of avoidable mortality was presented in a document 'Definition of avoidable mortality' [23] at the end of 2011.

The Members of Eurostat's Working Group of Public Health Statistics approved the list of diseases and age groups proposed by the Office for National Statistics of the United Kingdom. Hence, the Eurostat 'satellite lists' Task Force tested this proposed selection of causes of death by Delphi method; unfortunately, those results are not disseminated. The final EUROSTAT Satellite List defining causes of death considered as amenable or preventable is available at Eurostat web page [24]. We present the list of causes considered to be amenable in **Table 2**.

As one should notice, the development of concept of avoidable mortality has been considerably influenced by the evidence from clinical research studies or consultation that has confirmed the impact of health care or public health interventions on declining mortality. However, a considered time period has played an important role in creating the unique list of selected diseases, because medical knowledge and technology have advanced over time what subsequently has an impact on inclusion or exclusion criteria by which a list of amenable or preventable causes of death is made. Therefore, the lists of causes of death amenable to health care need to be regularly updated in relation to current medical practice.

3.3. Office for national statistics in England

Although avoidable mortality has been investigated for the last four decades, there is still small consensus among researchers about how to define it. Last precise definitions of the concept are presented by the Office for National Statistics in England [25]. Following definitions were developed through an iterative public consultation running in 2015.

3.3.1. Avoidable mortality

Avoidable deaths are all those defined as preventable, amenable (treatable) or both, where each death is counted only once; where a cause of death is both preventable and amenable, all deaths from that cause are counted in both categories when they are presented separately.

3.3.2. Amenable mortality

A death is amenable (treatable) if, in the light of medical knowledge and technology at the time of death, all or most deaths from that cause (subject to age limits if appropriate) could be avoided through good quality healthcare.

3.3.3. Preventable mortality

A death is preventable if, in the light of understanding of the determinants of health at time of death, all or most deaths from that cause (subject to age limits if appropriate) could be avoided by public health interventions in the broadest sense.

4. Analysis

In our analysis, we examine the impact of the lists of causes of death on amenable mortality by country, sex and cause of death. We compare the results of amenable mortality across the European Union (EU) countries calculated by the four lists of causes of death. Then, we are interested whether the two latest developed lists (AMIEHS and EUROSTAT) have a statistically significant impact on amenable mortality in Slovakia identifying the most influential group of diseases.

4.1. Data and methods

This section introduces what kind of dataset and methods are applied on the estimation of age-standardised amenable death rates when comparing the EU countries. It also includes information how significances of the results have been tested.

4.1.1. Data

Our main source of mortality data is the raw data files of the WHO Mortality Database, where the causes of death are coded using the ICD-10 classification at fourth digit level by five-year age groups. We conduct analysis on data from 2014, as it is the latest available time point. The data in the required structure for calculation of amenable mortality are available for 19 EU countries, while other EU countries do not meet the requirements of this analysis due to data incompleteness at some age groups. We select causes of death that are proposed by the Nolte and McKee, Tobias and Yeh, AMIEHS, EUROSTAT's list regardless to the age limit. Statistical database of the United Nations Economic Commission for Europe is the main source for data on mid-year population at the age groups. For comparison of mortality across EU countries, we adopt the European standard population by age groups according to the last revision in 2012, proceeding in 2013 [26].

4.1.2. Methods

We estimate age-standardised amenable death rates per 100,000 population by the direct method of standardisation to overcome an effect from variations in the age and sex structure across countries. First, the age and sex-specific death rates for the given causes of death are calculated in each examined country. Second, the age-specific death rate and the European standard population for each age interval are multiplied, and these results are summed. Finally, this sum is divided by the total standard population, in our case 100,000, to calculate the age-standardised death rate [27].

Two directly standardised rates calculated by the same standard population can be compared, and differences tested for statistical significance. To determine an association of countries' rank order according to the standardised death rates between the lists each other, we run a Spearman rank-order correlation with statistical significance tests. Probability values are computed from a *t*-distribution with N-2 degrees of freedom.

To find out whether age-standardised rates of amenable mortality based on the two lists are significantly different by sex and causes of death in Slovakia, we calculate 95% confidence intervals that are equivalent to statistical tests. As a general rule, a difference is statistically significance if a confidence interval around rate non-overlap with the interval around another [28]. Calculations are made using statistical software R Studio.

4.2. Between-list differences of amenable mortality across the European Union countries

This section compares the results of age standardised death rates across the European Union countries based on data from 2014 using the four evolutionarily most recent selections of amenable diagnoses. We tested the six null hypothesis statements (H_0) against the six alternative hypotheses (H_1):

- H_0: There is no association between the standardised death rates calculated by Nolte and McKee's list and the standardised death rates calculated by Tobias and Yeh's list.
- H_1: There is an association between the standardised death rates calculated by Nolte and McKee's list and the standardised death rates calculated by Tobias and Yeh's list.
- H_0: There is no association between the standardised death rates calculated by Nolte and McKee's list and the standardised death rates calculated by AMIEHS's list.
- H_1: There is an association between the standardised death rates calculated by Nolte and McKee's list and the standardised death rates calculated by AMIEHS's list.
- H_0: There is no association between the standardised death rates calculated by Nolte and McKee's list and the standardised death rates calculated by EUROSTAT's list.
- H_1: There is an association between the standardised death rates calculated by Nolte and McKee's list and the standardised death rates calculated by EUROSTAT's list.
- H_0: There is no association between the standardised death rates calculated by Tobias and Yeh's list and the standardised death rates calculated by AMIEHS's list.
- H_1: There is an association between the standardised death rates calculated by Tobias and Yeh's list and the standardised death rates calculated by AMIEHS's list.
- H_0: There is no association between the standardised death rates calculated by Tobias and Yeh's list and the standardised death rates calculated by EUROSTAT's list.
- H_1: There is an association between the standardised death rates calculated by Tobias and Yeh's list and the standardised death rates calculated by EUROSTAT's list.
- H_0: There is no association between the standardised death rates calculated by AMIEHS's list and the standardised death rates calculated by EUROSTAT's list.
- H_1: There is an association between the standardised death rates calculated by AMIEHS's list and the standardised death rates calculated by EUROSTAT's list.

Table 3 reports the Spearman's rank correlation matrix with a statistical significance of correlation coefficients. All calculated probability values achieved a value of $p < 0.001$, what means that we can reject the null hypothesis. In other words, despite any concept of amenable mortality applied, there is a significant very strong positive correlation of the standardised death rates. Generally, the Spearman's correlation test calculated on standardised death rates of amenable causes using the Nolte and McKee, Tobias and Yeh, AMIEHS or EUROSTAT's concepts, shows that the *rank order of countries does not change significantly*.

	sdr_NOLTE & McKEE	sdr_TOBIAS & YEH	sdr_AMIEHS	sdr_EUROSTAT
sdr_NOLTE & McKEE	1.0000000	0.9403509	0.9877193	0.9807018
p-value	*8.377e-06*	*4.836e-06*	*8.402e-06*	*8.267e-06*
sdr_TOBIAS & YEH	0.9403509	1.0000000	0.9333333	0.9456140
p-value	*4.836e-06*	*8.377e-06*	*3.74e-06*	*5.562e-06*
sdr_AMIEHS	0.9877193	0.9333333	1.0000000	0.9894737
p-value	*8.402e-06*	*3.74e-06*	*8.377e-06*	*8.418e-06*
sdr_EUROSTAT	0.9807018	0.9456140	0.9894737	1.0000000
p-value	*8.267e-06*	*5.562e-06*	*8.418e-06*	*8.377e-06*

Note: Probability values computed from a t distribution with N-2 degrees of freedom. $N = 19$.
Source: Own calculation using R Studio.

Table 3. Spearman's rank correlation matrix with *p*-values calculated for standardised death rates (sdr) by country based on the four lists of amenable causes, 2014.

These results are depicted in **Figure 1**. The four lists provide different levels of amenable mortality rates for countries; however, the rank order of countries is very similar. In 2014, France accounted for the best results of amenable mortality obtained from the all examined lists, ranged from 61 to 79 deaths per 100,000 population. On the other hand, the worst rate was recorded in Romania, 275 per 100,000 calculated by Nolte and McKee's list, as well as an average of 309 deaths per 100,000 in Latvia estimated by three remaining lists.

Generally, the standardised death rates for EU-19 calculated by Eurostat's list were 40.5% higher than rates calculated by Nolte and McKee's list. On the other hand, the rates calculated according to the lists of Tobias and Yeh or AMIEHS were nearly the same, 161 per 100,000, 162 per 100,000, respectively. Using the Nolte and McKee's list, the amenable mortality rates for EU-19 reached the lowest value, 128 deaths per 100,000 population. The standard deviations (not shown in this document) expressing the rate of variability of standardised amenable death rates between lists, gained the highest values in Eastern European countries (Latvia, Lithuania, Slovakia, Hungary, Romania, the Czech Republic, Poland), along with Denmark, Estonia, the United Kingdom, Croatia, had still standard deviations above the average of EU-19. A gradual decline of the variation in amenable mortality rates, below an average of EU-19, was demonstrated in the Netherlands, Germany, Luxembourg, Malta, Sweden, Finland, Spain and France.

Observed between-list differences of the level of standardised amenable death rates in the EU countries are due to discrepancies in selected diseases and age limits. However, when assessing the effectiveness of health systems in examined countries, it has not changed significantly.

4.3. The impact of AMIEHS and EUROSTAT's list on amenable mortality by cause of death in Slovakia

The analysis examines whether age-standardised rates of amenable mortality based on AMIEHS or EUROSTAT's list are significantly different by sex and causes of death in Slovakia. We apply both lists on data for 2014.

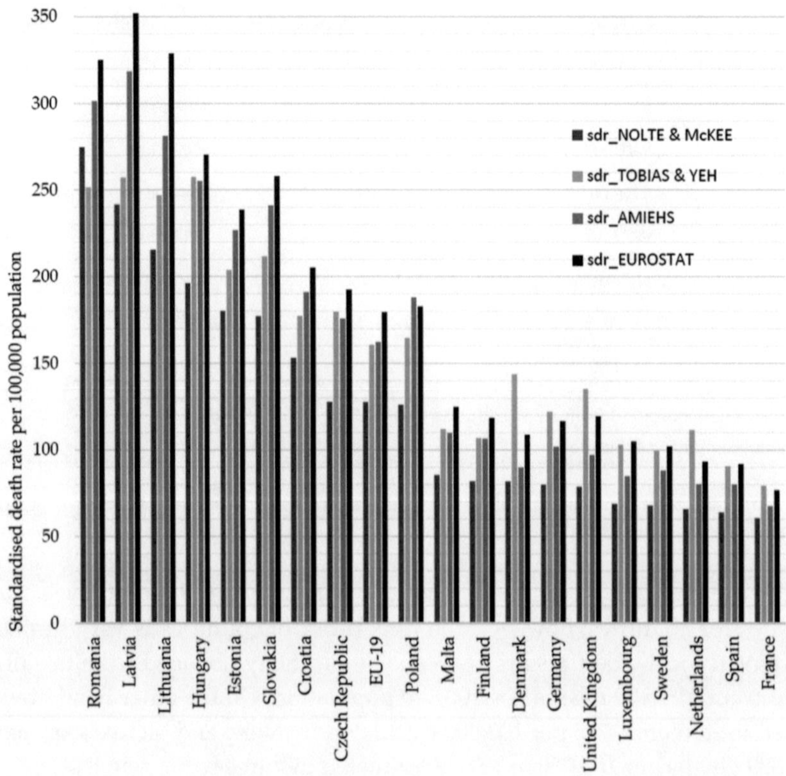

Figure 1. Amenable mortality across the European Union countries by the four lists of causes of death, 2014. *Source*: Own calculation based on the data from WHO mortality database.

In Slovakia, there was a considerable increase in the number of deaths considered amenable, from 9325 by the AMIEHS's list to 10,451 under the EUROSTAT's list. Of the additional 1126 deaths, 753 were for men and 373 for women. The increase occurred in all age groups, mostly after 55 years of age, and also not negligibly in the children aged from 0 to 4 years. The majority of the increase was due to the inclusion of respiratory diseases in the EUROSTAT's list that contributed 585 deaths of the 1126 deaths. The increase in the number of amenable deaths revealed that the total amenable mortality rates, as well as the rates for men and women, calculated by EUROSTAT's list were *significantly higher* (by 14.2% for men and 11.3% for women) than the rates under the AMIEHS's list. Generally, a difference is statistically significance if a confidence interval around rate non-overlap with the interval around another (**Table 4**).

Table 5 reflects the age-standardised amenable mortality rates, based on the AMIEHS and EUROSTAT's list (with 95% confidence intervals) by broad cause group in Slovakia, 2014.

Besides the inclusion of respiratory diseases in the EUROSTAT's list, the increases in the number of deaths were also due to the inclusions of epilepsy contributing 96 deaths, diabetes with 37 deaths and misadventures to patients during surgical and medical care adding 15 deaths. Thus,

	AMIEHS's list				EUROSTAT's list			
Sex	Number of deaths	Rate per 100,000 population	Lower 95% CI	Upper 95% CI	Number of deaths	Rate per 100,000 population	Lower 95% CI	Upper 95% CI
Men	5730	290.3	282.6	298.0	6483	331.4	323.9	338.9
Women	3595	150.1	145.2	155.0	3968	167	162.3	171.7
Total	9325	212.6	208.2	217.0	10,451	240.1	235.9	244.3

Note: CI, confidence interval.

Source: Own calculation based on the data from WHO mortality database.

Table 4. Number of deaths and standardised amenable death rates based on AMIEHS or EUROSTAT's list in Slovakia, 2014.

	AMIEHS's list				EUROSTAT's list			
Cause group	Number of deaths	Rate per 100,000	Lower 95% CI	Upper 95% CI	Number of deaths	Rate per 100,000	Lower 95% CI	Upper 95% CI
All amenable causes	9325	212.6	208.2	217.0	10,451	240.1	235.9	244.3
Infectious disease	1	0.02	0.0	0.06	159	3.5	3.0	4.0
Neoplasms	2020	44.6	42.6	46.6	2,324	52.2	50.2	54.2
Diabetes mellitus (type 2)	nc	nc	nc	nc	37	1.1	0.9	1.3
Ischaemic heart disease	4184	96.6	93.6	99.6	4184	96.6	93.6	99.6
Other circulatory disease	2650	61.3	58.9	63.7	2276	53.5	51.5	55.5
Respiratory diseases	nc	nc	nc	nc	585	13.4	12.4	14.4
Surgical conditions	275	6.3	5.6	7.0	465	10.5	9.6	11.4
Congenital and perinatal conditions	195	3.7	3.2	4.2	310	5.7	5.1	6.3
Epilepsy and status epilepticus	nc	nc	nc	nc	96	2.0	1.6	2.4
Misadventures to patients during surgical and medical care	nc	nc	nc	nc	15	0.3	0.1	0.5

Note: nc, non-classified.

Source: Own calculation based on the data from WHO mortality database.

Table 5. Standardised amenable mortality rates based on the AMIEHS and EUROSTAT's list (with 95% confidence intervals) by broad cause group in Slovakia, 2014.

additional causes of death included in the EUROSTAT's list accounted for 12.1%. A largest share in both lists is presented by ischaemic heart disease representing 44.9% under the AMIEHS's list and 40% in the EUROSTAT's list. However, standardised death rate of ischaemic heart disease has not changed when comparing the two lists. The other circulatory disease reported the statistically significant decrease of standardised death rates by 14.1% in the EUROSTAT's list contrary to the AMIEHS's list that was due to the exclusion of heart failure from the group. However, heart failure represented a substantial cause accounted for 14.1% in the group of other circulatory disease under the AMIEHS's list. In spite of the fact that infectious disease reflected the lowest numbers of deaths in the both lists, they recorded the largest statistically significant increase under the EUROSTAT's list because of the additional causes of death (tuberculosis, hepatitis C, selected invasive bacterial and protozoal infections) to the HIV contained in the AMIEHS's list. Moreover, in the HIV cause group, there was the extension of the age limit on the all age groups, whereas the age limit 0–74 years was included in the AMIEHS's list. In the neoplasms cause group, there was a statistically significant increase in the number of deaths by 15% mainly because of the addition of malignant neoplasms of skin and bladder cancer to the EUROSTAT's list and the shortness of the upper age limit of leukaemia. Finally, the standardised death rates for the surgical, congenital and perinatal conditions increased significantly under the EUROSTAT's list by 69.1 and 59%, respectively, mainly due to the inclusion of some surgical conditions (acute abdomen, appendicitis, intestinal obstruction, etc.) and the extension of the scope of congenital malformations to the overall 17 chapters of ICD-10.

5. Discussion about conceptual problems

While avoidable mortality seems to be an innovative indicator for measuring the effectiveness of medical services, it has number of limitations resulting from the data sets relevance, as well as the concept itself. It is very important to clearly distinguish between the meaning of the avoidable, amenable and preventable mortality. These terms are often mixed up what lead to the confusion in their interpretation. For example, interpreting the decrease in avoidable mortality only such as observing a positive impact of treatment can mask an effective introduction of public health interventions.

Since health care system characteristics as well as their levels of accessibility vary from country to country, there is an absence of international agreement on the uniform selection of causes of death and age limit in the cross-country comparison. Although the methodologies strictly do not distinguish causes of death or age limits for men and women separately, it would be useful to further develop the concept of avoidable mortality differentiating age limits for males and females to reflect the greater longevity of women. In our complementary analyses [29, 30], we found that amenable mortality is generally higher in men than in women, irrespective of the four concept used. The differences between men and women are much higher in countries with higher amenable mortality than in countries with lower amenable death rates. These facts are consistent with the findings of a research project AMIEHS. It declares that the disparity between male and female premature mortality is partially determined by the provision of health care.

http://dx.doi.org/10.5772/67818

This concept does not take into account the fact that different countries do not have the same health care resources needed for effective treatment, such as available new required technologies, medical skills or sufficient number of professionals. Additionally, it is not monitored whether countries secure distribution and dissemination of the necessary resources. For this reason, avoidable mortality should be interpreted in the context of many other available characteristics of health care system performance in the country. Hence, avoidable mortality can be an effective indicator in the assessment of progress achieved by the country in a certain time period.

The lack of resources can lead to the increase of disease prevalence that is not adjusted in the amenable mortality indicator. For example, based on our previous study [31], Slovakia has gained the worst values of standardised mortality rate of ischaemic heart disease (above 500 deaths per 100,000) across the European countries in the long term. In this case, we should find out whether incidence or prevalence of ischaemic heart disease was not significantly increased in the examined time period, otherwise, we might interpret mistakenly a decrease of the quality of health care by an ineffective treatment of ischaemic heart disease or prevention programs in Slovakia. It is useful to assess the individual diagnosis in the given countries, as the countries with high levels of avoidable mortality tend to have a high level of mortality in individual cases.

Additionally, we see a disadvantage of variations in diagnostic practices and cause of death coding between countries, what also impacts both on international comparison and national level assessment of amenable mortality. We found out that by 2009, causes of death were coded at the third digit level (e.g. B17), while since 2010 at the fourth digit level (e.g. B171). These discrepancies may have led to the distortion of comparison of causes of death over time. The use of EUROSTAT's list before 2010 could overvalue the number of deaths, since the whole group of 'other acute viral hepatitis' (B17) would have been considered instead of 'hepatitis C' (B171).

One of the reasons for the benefits of composing the avoidable mortality concept at the national level, supported by previous studies of AMIEHS and Office for National Statistics, may be a time lag between the improved of health care services or introduction of a public health prevention program and a corresponding decrease of amenable mortality. Based on AMIEHS, a time lag was 7 years, while the Office for National Statistics in England suggests that selection of avoidable causes of death should be updated every 3 years.

We have to realise that variations in avoidable mortality are also influenced by socio-economic factors, which can mask the impact of health care system effectiveness. We consider as the main limitation of the concept of avoidable mortality the fact that many factors beyond the health system influence mortality and an indicator of avoidable mortality does not capture many of them. Therefore, cross-country comparison based only on this indicator can be biased. Other complementary indicators such as health services supply, health expenditures or gains in quality of life should be used in combination with avoidable mortality indicators to assess the effectiveness of the health care system.

Permanent evaluation of the concept based on the epidemiological studies, availability of health technologies and interventions supported by empirical evidence could help create an effective tool for measurement avoidable mortality mainly at the national level.

6. Conclusion

The aim of this study is to compare the impact of the four latest lists of causes of death on the age-standardised amenable death rates across the European Union countries in 2014. Our results showed that the rank order of countries does not change significantly, even though we applied Nolte and McKee, Tobias and Yeh, AMIEHS or EUROSTAT's concepts. In addition, we analysed whether age-standardised rates of amenable mortality based on AMIEHS or EUROSTAT's list are significantly different by sex and causes of death in Slovakia. We revealed that amenable mortality rates calculated by sex under the EUROSTAT's list were significantly higher than to the rates under the AMIEHS's list. This finding suggests that the structure of diseases together with the given age limits significantly influence the value of standardised amenable death rates, and hence, it is beneficial to develop the concept of amenable mortality at the national level in the light of actual availability of medical skills and effective treatments in the country.

Our results can serve as a valuable platform for revising the 'Strategic framework of health system in the Slovak Republic' aimed at increasing effectiveness of the health care system. Accurate quantification of the impacts of morbidity, comorbidities, socio-economic factors, lifestyle, health behaviours and others factors provide an extensive support in the interpretation of the development of avoidable mortality not only in international comparisons, but also in the development Slovak's own avoidable mortality methodology.

Acknowledgements

This chapter was created within the project supported by the Scientific Grant Agency of the Ministry of Education, Science, Research and Sport of the Slovak Republic 1/0945/17 Research of the economic quantification of marketing processes aimed at increasing the value for the patient, multi-dimensional analyses of the marketing mix of health facilities and quantification of their importance in the process of establishing a system to measure the quality and effectiveness of health system in the Slovak Republic. The authors thank to the National Health Information Centre of the Slovak Republic for providing access to the central mortality database for the explored period as well as the other studied data along with the Statistical Office of the Slovak Republic. They also acknowledge the Ministry of Health of the Slovak Republic for its cooperation in creation of the new conceptions and methodologies and for its support of our research activities.

Author details

Beata Gavurova* and Tatiana Vagasova

*Address all correspondence to: beata.gavurova@tuke.sk

Faculty of Economics, Technical University of Košice, Němcovej, Košice, Slovakia

References

[1] European Commission. Development of a Methodology for Collection and Analysis of Data on Efficiency and Effectiveness in Health Care Provision [Internet]. 2005. Available from: http://www.basys.de/aktuelles/sha-efficiency.pdf [Accessed: 2016-12-06]

[2] Joumard I, Hoeller P, André C, Nicq C. Health Care Systems: Efficiency and Policy Settings. Paris: OECD Publishing; 2010. 212 p. DOI: 10.1787/9789264094901-en

[3] Rutstein D, Berenberg W, Chalmers T, Child C, Fishman A, Perrin E. Measuring the Quality of Medical Care. N Engl J Med. 1976; 294:582-588. DOI: 10.1056/NEJM197603112941104

[4] Charlton JR, Hartley RM, Silver R, Holland WW. Geographical Variation in Mortality from Conditions Amenable to Medical Intervention in England and Wales. Lancet. 1983; 26:691-696. DOI: 10.1016/S0140-6736(83)91981-5

[5] Poikolainen K, Eskola J. Health Services Resources and their Relation to Mortality from Causes Amenable to Health Care Intervention: A Cross-National Study. Int J Epidemiol. 1988; 17:86-89. DOI: 10.1093/ije/17.1.86

[6] Mackenbach JP, Kunst AE, Looman CW, Habbema JD, van der Maas PJ. Regional Differences in Mortality from Conditions Amenable to Medical Intervention in the Netherlands: A Comparison of Four Time Periods. J Epidemiol Community Health. 1998; 42: 325-332.

[7] Holland W, editor. European Community Atlas of 'Avoidable Death'. Commission of the European Communities Health Services Research Series No.3. Oxford: Oxford University Press; 1988. 304 p.

[8] Holland W, editor. European Community atlas of 'avoidable death' (2nd ed. Vol. II). Commission of the European Communities Health Services Research Series No. 3. Oxford: Oxford University Press; 1993.

[9] Holland W, editor. European Community Atlas of 'Avoidable Death' 1985-89. Oxford: Oxford University Press; 1997.

[10] Westerling R, Smedby B. The European Community 'Avoidable Death Indicators' in Sweden 1974-1985. Int J Epidemiol. 1992; 21:502-510. DOI: 10.1093/ije/21.3.502

[11] Westerling R. Indicators of "Avoidable" Mortality in Health Administrative Areas in Sweden 1974-1985. Scand J Public Health. 1993; 21:176-187.

[12] Westerling R, Gullberg A, Rosén M. Socioeconomic Differences in 'Avoidable' Mortality in Sweden 1986-1990. Int J Epidemiol. 1996; 25: 560-567. DOI: 10.1093/ije/25.3.560

[13] Simonato L, Ballard T, Bellini P, Winkelmann R. Avoidable Mortality in Europe 1955-1994: A Plea for Prevention. J Epidemiol Community Health. 1998; 52:624-630.

[14] Tobias M, Jackson G. Avoidable Mortality in New Zealand, 1981-97. Aust N Z J Public Health. 2001; 25:12-20. DOI: 10.1111/j.1467-842X.2001.tb00543.x

[15] Nolte E, McKee M. Does Health Care Save Lives? Avoidable Mortality Revisited. London: The Nuffield Trust; 2004. 138 p.

[16] Nolte E, McKee M. Measuring the Health of Nations: Updating an Earlier Analysis. Health Affairs. 2008; 27:58-71. DOI: 10.1377/hlthaff.27.1.58

[17] Tobias M, Yeh L. How Much does Health Care Contribute to Health Gain and to Health Inequality? Trends in Amenable Mortality in New Zealand 1981-2004. Aust N Z J Public Health. 2009; 33:70-78. DOI: 10.1111/j.1753-6405.2009.00342.x

[18] Plug I, Hoffmann R, Mackenbach J, editors. AMIEHS: Avoidable Mortality in the European Union: Towards Better Indicators for the Effectiveness of Health Systems [Internet]. 2011. Available from: http://amiehs.lshtm.ac.uk/[Accessed: 2016-12-08]

[19] Eurostat. Amenable and Preventable Deaths Statistics [Internet]. 2013. Available from: http://ec.europa.eu/eurostat/statistics-explained/index.php/Amenable_and_preventable_deaths_statistics [Accessed: 2016-12-08]

[20] AMIEHS. Atlas of Amenable Mortality [Internet]. 2011. Available from: https://survey.erasmusmc.nl/amiehs/atlas.html [Accessed: 2016-12-11]

[21] Office for National Statistics. Definitions of Avoidable Mortality [Internet]. 2011. Available from: http://www.ons.gov.uk/ons/about-ons/consultations/closed-consultations/2011/definitions-of-avoidable-mortality/consultation-on-definitions-of-avoidable-mortality.pdf [Accessed: 2016-12-11]

[22] Office for National Statistics. Responses to the Public Consultation on Definitions of Avoidable Mortality [Internet]. 2011. Available from: http://www.ons.gov.uk/ons/about-ons/consultations/closed-consultations/2011/definitions-of-avoidable-mortality/summary-of-responses-to-the-consultation-on-definitions-of-avoidable-mortality.pdf [Accessed: 2016-12-11]

[23] Office for National Statistics. Definition of Avoidable Mortality [Internet]. 2011. Available from: https://www.google.sk/url?sa=t&rct=j&q=&esrc=s&source=web&cd=1&cad=rja&uact=8&ved=0ahUKEwihhqzn1-_RAhXFcRQKHWXlBkcQFggdMAA&url=https%3A%2F%2Fwww.ons.gov.uk%2Fons%2Fabout-ons%2Fget-involved%2Fconsultations%2Farchived-consultations%2F2011%2Fdefinitions-of-avoidablemortality%2Fdefinition-of-avoidable-mortality.pdf&usg=AFQjCNEXtusGzTcBppvdr4qjPHBYFOKydg&sig2=zehJCe1STgcyDkpQWb7vfw&bvm=bv.145822982,d.d24 [Accessed: 2016-12-11]

[24] Eurostat 'Satellite List' Task Force. Specifications of the Public Health Theme Tables [Internet]. 2013. Available from: http://ec.europa.eu/eurostat/cache/metadata/Annexes/hlth_cdeath_esms_an4.pdf [Accessed: 2016-12-11]

[25] Office for National Statistics. Statistical Bulletin: Avoidable Mortality in England and Wales: 2014 [Internet]. 2016. Available from: https://www.ons.gov.uk/peoplepopulationandcommunity/healthandsocialcare/causesofdeath/bulletins/avoidablemortalityinenglandandwales/2014 [Accessed: 2016-12-12]

[26] European Commission. Revision of the European Standard Population. Report of Eurostat's Task Force. Luxembourg: Publications Office of the European Union; 2013. 128 p. DOI: 10.2785/11470

[27] Curtin LR, Klein RJ. Direct Standardization (Age-Adjusted Death Rates). Statistical Notes. USA: Centers for Disease Control and Prevention; 1995. 11 p.

[28] Washington State Department of Health. Guidelines for Using Confidence Intervals for Public Health Assessment [Internet]. 2012. Available from: http://www.doh.wa.gov/Portals/1/Documents/5500/ConfIntGuide.pdf [Accessed: 2016-12-12]

[29] Gavurová B, Vagašová T. Avoidable mortality in Slovakia. Trends between 1994 and 2013. eXclusive J. 2014; 2:52-62.

[30] Gavurová B, Vagašová T. The significance of amenable mortality quantification for financing the health system in Slovakia. Procedia Econ Finance. 2015; 32:77-86. DOI: 10.1016/S2212-5671(15)01367-2

[31] Gavurová B, Vagašová T. Regional differences of standardised mortality rates for ischemic heart diseases in the Slovak Republic for the period 1996-2013 in the context of income inequality. Health Econ Rev. 2016; 6(21):1-12. DOI: 10.1186/s13561-016-0099-1

Chapter 6

The Efficiency of Post-Communist Countries' Health Systems

Justyna Kujawska

Additional information is available at the end of the chapter

http://dx.doi.org/10.5772/67817

Abstract

Health-care costs are a major financial burden for the transition economies, which have experienced rapidly increasing demand for health-care services. The former communist countries of the Central and Eastern Europe and Central Asia needed to reform the financing of their health-care systems and make efforts to strengthen the role of primary care while limiting the role of hospital care. The growing health needs and, consequently, costs resulted in the increased attention paid to the performance of health systems. The aim of this chapter is to determine the efficiency of health systems in post-communist countries. The data envelopment analysis method was used. The effective health systems were identified and recommendations for the inefficient countries were formulated.

Keywords: health-care efficiency, post-communist countries, data envelopment analysis

1. Introduction

At the turn of the twentieth and twenty-first centuries, both insurance- and provision-based health systems underwent profound changes. Rising health-care costs became a current economic, social and political problem. During this period, the post-communist countries transformed their economies from command to market systems. Also, the health systems were transformed from the Semashko model to insurance model.

All countries regardless of their level of economic development endeavour to improve the quality and accessibility of health services, which requires objective and reliable assessment of the functioning of their health systems. Both policymakers and society expect the best possible outputs of the health systems, due to the relatively large expenditures allocated for their functioning [1].

The efficiency of public organizations has become an area of practical measurement and scientific research. The evaluation of efficiency in terms of quantity should be the basic premise of making economic decisions. The more accurate it is, the more accurate and relevant are the information it provides.

Assessment of health systems should be carried out in two dimensions, where the *effectiveness* of the system reflects its success in achieving its objectives, whereas the *efficiency* reflects the success of transformation of inputs into outcomes [2]. In this study, the latter approach prevails.

International comparative studies of health systems often use, among other medical resources, health-care spending measured as the share of gross domestic product (GDP) or per capita. It should be noted, however, that a constant share of health-care spending in GDP over time does not mean that spending is constant, but rather that changes in health-care spending are proportional to GDP changes [3].

Controlling spending on health care and the system of its financing is a priority aspect in designing public policy. The interest in this issue has increased in recent years as a result of the economic crisis and the need for financing health care with budget funds or by increasing the share of patients' private out-of-pocket expenditure [4].

An illness can cause lack of economic security both directly and indirectly. For those without or with partial health insurance, medical expenses can be devastating, leading to debt or opting out of treatment at the expense of worsening health in the future. Health insurance may cover different options, and even the insured individuals may incur high costs, paying directly for some services or medicines.

It should be noted, however, that the transformation of command economies proved more complicated than it was originally thought. Job insecurity, social inequality and the decline in spending on social and health insurance after the economic collapse contributed to the deterioration of health-care outcomes.

The purpose of this chapter is to determine the efficiency of health-care systems of post-communist countries. The study was conducted for the 28 countries of the former Eastern bloc for the years 2000 and 2013 using the method of data envelopment analysis (DEA). Averages of health indicators for the 16 economically developed countries of Western Europe were used as a benchmark.

The originality of this approach consists in focusing research on post-communist countries, for which a small number of studies are carried out, as well as on conducting a broad discussion of projections, i.e. the necessary measures that must be taken to enable the countries which were in the Soviet sphere of influence after the Second World War to achieve such health results as in the case of the most developed European countries. Conducting research in multiple years allowed for verifying whether the actions taken within the framework of economy transition influence also the health systems.

2. Financing of health care in post-communist countries

The post-communist countries of Central and Eastern Europe and Central Asia (CEECA) transformed their economies, which included the transformation of health-care systems from the Semashko model to insurance (social health insurance, SHI) or budget (national health service, NHS) approach. Therefore, it seems necessary to measure the effectiveness of the introduced changes and assess the outcomes of health care.

The health-care system in the centralized economy of the Soviet Union was plagued by chronic underfunding, antiquated and deteriorating facilities, inadequate supplies and outmoded equipment, poor morale and no incentives for health-care workers to boost the productivity, as well as consumer dissatisfaction. Health statistics reveal poor life expectancy and high mortality rates, with striking disparities among the individual republics [5].

The post-communist economies are catching up with most developed countries, but the gap in economic development remains very significant and is especially evident in the level of gross domestic product per capita and its derivatives, e.g. health-care spending per capita. The differences are also visible in the achieved health outcomes.

Health-care systems are usually funded from sources such as taxes, public and private health insurance contributions or patients' out-of-pocket payments [6].

The percentage of health-care financing from public funds is used as an indicator enabling the assessment of the role of the state in this area. The strong role of the state, reflected by a high level of funding from the public budget, points to the elimination of inequalities in access to medical services. On the other hand, the percentage of out-of-pocket patient payments or private insurance allows for the assessment of the financial burden imposed on households in the event of necessity to use health services [7]. The high level of out-of-pocket expenses increases the difficulty of obtaining medical assistance for people with lower incomes and lower health status [8]. The countries with a low share of public expenditure should aim at reducing the level of out-of-pocket payments in favour of prepaid private insurance. This way, the public could finance health services in a more predictable manner, without facing the problematic, sudden necessity to find the funds to pay for treatment in case of an unforeseen illness. The large share of out-of-pocket payments in the case of the poorer social groups exacerbates the risk of the so-called catastrophic expenditure, leading to impoverishment or abandonment of often necessary medical services. Moving away from the out-of-pocket patients' payments towards prepaid private insurance reduces the possibility of a financial catastrophe [9–11].

Classifying health systems in post-communist countries according to their financial agents indicates that in the Central Europe (CE) health care is financed mainly by health insurance contributions and in Eastern Europe and Central Asia (EECA) mainly from taxes and out-of-pocket payments of households. The average share of total public expenditure in the analysed countries of Central and Eastern Europe and Central Asia amounted to 58.8% in the analysed years. In 2013, the average share of public expenditure in the CE countries amounted to 66.0%, and in the EECA countries, it was equal to 43.5%. The share of funding from government social health insurance in general averaged 63.2% and increased by 5.8 percentage points (p.p.) over the period of 14 years. In the CE countries, it averaged 73.8%, and in the EECA countries, the average amounted to 29.7%. In contrast, only in the former Soviet Union, where the budget system prevails, SHI amounted to 36.3%. In most analysed countries, the share of private and out-of-pocket funding is high. The average share of private expenditure in total expenditure on health amounted to 41.2%—in the case of the CE countries, it amounted to 34.0%, and in the case of the EECA countries, it was equal to 56.5%. The share of out-of-pocket expenditure in private spending averaged 88.6%, while in the case of the CE countries, it was lower by 1.3 p.p., and in the EECA countries, it was higher by 4.2 p.p. In most post-communist countries, even those where public funding is very low, citizens do not show interest in additional health insurance. In 2013, private prepaid plans accounted for 6% of expenditure on average: 6.9% in the CE countries and 4% in the EECA countries. In the Central Europe, almost 50% of the Slovenian, 40% of Croatian, 7% of Hungarian and 4% Latvian population have prepaid private insurance. In the Eastern Europe and Central Asia, prepaid health insurance was used by 12% of Georgian, 6% of Armenian and Uzbek as well as 4% of Russian population.

The insurance type of health system is not the classic Bismarck model but its modification. The noticeable majority of Central Europe and Balkan peninsula adopted only the method of funding (health insurance contributions), while the organization and governance of health care are organized differently in each of the countries. The health systems in which there are several third-party payers operate in Czech Republic, Lithuania and Slovakia. Most mechanisms of the Bismarck model were introduced in the health-care system of the Czech Republic and Slovakia. The payers in the system are sickness funds, which conclude contracts with service providers. The patients are free to choose the insurance company, and the largest insurer in each of the countries has over 60% market share. In both countries, there are mechanisms of pooling and (re)allocation of contributions ex ante referred to as risk adjustment of contributions. Only in the Czech system, there is a mechanism to retrospective risk sharing [12]. In Lithuania, there are sickness funds, but their membership is territorial. There is no competition between insurers nor any mechanism of risk adjustment of contributions. On the other hand, health-care insurance systems with a single payer prevail in Albania, Bosnia and Herzegovina, Bulgaria, Estonia, Hungary, Macedonia, Moldova, Montenegro, Poland, Romania, Serbia and Slovenia. In the post-Soviet countries of Eastern Europe and Central Asia, centrally planned health systems with less public funding than in the countries of Central Europe prevail—the examples include Azerbaijan, Georgia and Tajikistan. The tendency of the public to purchase prepaid private insurance is not significant, which makes it difficult to access to health care due to lack of financial resources in households. In Kyrgyzstan and Russia, mandatory health insurance was introduced; however, these are supply systems financed from the budget, as in other countries not listed above.

Kyrgyzstan is the only example of a Central Asian country where the introduction of a health insurance system was successful. SHI is a system complementary in relation to budget financing and supplements public funding. In the analysed period, the share of public funds from health insurance increased. At the same time, a successful reform the health infrastructure was implemented—some facilities were closed, but the overall access to health care for all citizens was improved [13]. Despite the introduction of SHI in the Russian Federation and the initial successes, the reform of health-care financing eventually failed. In the 2000–2013 period, the share of public expenditure in the total expenditure on health care decreased—the fall included the funds from SHI.

It should also be noted that in all the post-communist countries, there were high informal payments and in-kind gifts from patients as compensation for the health-care workers' treatment efforts [14]. They were more prevalent in hospitals than in outpatient care. It is estimated that in some countries, they constitute up to 10–15% of private expenditure. Such payments and gifts are due to the lack of determination of a state-funded benefit package (in Armenia and Georgia) or the fact that the benefit package is very extensive but chronically underfunded (such as in Azerbaijan, the Russian Federation, Tajikistan and Ukraine) [15]. This practice has been limited but not eliminated, since the obvious reason for its occurrence is the relatively low salaries of health-care workers, often paid late. In some countries, the informal compensation is replaced by formal charges for health services.

3. Research on the efficiency of health-care systems

Measuring the efficiency of health-care systems is not an easy task, and the main difficulty is the correct measurement of the outcomes of the system operation. The most frequently used approach is based on the measurable indirect indicators of services, which by definition have a fundamental effect on the health of the population. The outcomes of the health-care system can be defined as the change in the state population health that can be attributed to health-care spending, e.g. life expectancy, infant mortality, inequality in access, incidence of certain diseases, etc. [1]. Although there may be some controversy as to the suitability of some of these variables as important outcomes of health care, most of the analyses conducted on the level of systems use life expectancy and infant mortality to assess the performance of health systems (e.g. Refs. [3, 16–19]). Infant mortality is not a dramatic problem in the developed countries. However, even among members of the Organisation for Economic Co-operation and Development (OECD), such as Mexico, Chile or Turkey, or in former Soviet republics such as Tajikistan, Turkmenistan or Uzbekistan, this indicator is still high. It is much easier to define the inputs, which, when used properly, determine the overall efficiency. Usually the resource approach is used, based on quantifiable inputs such as the number of physicians or available infrastructure (e.g. number of beds, diagnostic equipment, financial resources, etc.). It is also a common practice to base models on variables indirectly reflecting outputs and inputs, proxies, which is a consequence of the limited availability of relevant data [20].

Given the purpose of this chapter, the review of the literature focuses on the studies of the effectiveness of health systems conducted in the world, treating expenditure and its structure as input and using the DEA method.

The share of public spending in total health-care expenditure was included as one of the inputs in the study of differences in physicians' effectiveness of improving public health in OECD countries [21]. In addition, the analysis takes into account the number of physicians, the level of GDP per capita, the level of education of the society as well as environmental variables: the consumption of alcohol and smoking. The results were based on the life expectancy at birth and at 65 years of age and the number of years of life lost due to heart diseases (for men and women separately) and infant mortality. These variables are commonly used as the outcomes of health-care systems.

The analysis carried out for the 165 countries for which data were available in the WHO database shows that the share of public health-care spending and the size of health-care spending in public budgets are two factors positively related to the functioning of health-care systems [1]. A modified DEA model was used, allowing for the introduction of weight restrictions, which increases the discriminatory strength of the method. Two kinds of input, the total expenditure on health per capita and the expected length of education (as an environmental factor), as well as two outputs—good-health life expectancy and the number of years lost due to disability or premature death—were taken into account. The level of public financing reached 64% in the most effective countries from the sample, whereas in the least efficient ones, the public funding did not exceed 50%. It can be said that in the countries whose governments show commitment to the development and financing of health-care systems, the available resources are used more effectively while allowing for achieving adequate health outcomes.

A similar approach to creating models of technical effectiveness of health-care systems can be found in other publications. In the case of OECD countries, a study of the effectiveness of health-care resources usage, measured by such parameters as the number of physicians, the number of beds per 1000 inhabitants, the number of units of magnetic resonance imaging (MRI) per million inhabitants or health-care spending as the percentage of GDP, was conducted [16]. The authors adopted infant mortality rate and life expectancy at birth as the results of such inputs. The extended analyses also take into account the social and environmental factors, such as the Gini coefficient, school expectancy or tobacco consumption. Two models were built separately for each outcome. Two countries, Iceland and Luxembourg, were eliminated from the analysis due to missing data. An interesting observation is that among the fully efficient countries, such as Sweden, Norway and Japan, there are also those with weak health outcomes, such as Turkey and Mexico. This is due to the fact that the poor performance of these countries is related to their low consumption of resources. This shows that at every level of the achieved health outcomes, a country may be technically efficient or inefficient as regards the use of its resources.

It is emphasized that the maximization of health system outcomes requires a good understanding of the factors included in the health production function. Such an analysis can help the decision makers to understand the conditions for a more efficient operation of health-care systems better. In their study [19], they used output-oriented BCC and super efficiency models, both with variable returns to scale. As outcomes, the infant mortality rate (IMR) and life expectancy at birth were adopted. As inputs, the number of doctors per 1000 inhabitants, the number of hospital beds per 1000 inhabitants, health expenditure per capita, GDP per capita and consumption of fruit and vegetables per capita were adopted. Two models were built, with different inputs in order to achieve different objectives of the study, i.e. to differentiate the production function, which is mainly based on the expenditure deemed discretionary, that is possible to be controlled by the health system, and the production function, which includes the inputs that are non-discretionary, that is outside of the possibility of control by the health-care system. The authors also conducted a regression analysis of the results of measurements of the efficiency, using such explanatory variables as, fat intake as a proxy for the style of life of residents and their behaviours and the unemployment rates and the Gini index as the variables representing the degree of the challenges associated with changes in the social environment affecting the health of the population. Based on the results of the analysis, it can be determined that health-care systems in nine countries with large and stable economies were identified as efficient when the evaluation of their functioning was based on discretionary inputs (controlled by health systems), whereas inefficiency was observed when the assessment was based on non-discretionary inputs that are largely beyond the control of health-care systems.

Some publications that apply to researching the effectiveness of health systems in post-communist countries are discussed below. The analysis covered the health outcomes of Croatia and Slovak Republic in the context of other countries from Central and Eastern Europe (CEE). Although the overall health spending efficiency of the CEE countries is on par with that of the OECD, substantial inefficiencies occur in the process of transforming intermediate health inputs into health outcomes. High levels of cost-effectiveness reflect relatively low prices for labour; hence despite the low level of spending, the resources of health care are relatively high. Given the favourable ratio of public to private spending and available resources, it can be said that the health outcomes of the populations could be improved. The authors propose a stimulated development of private insurance by restricting the basic benefit package provided by public spending. Also the costs of pharmaceuticals should be restricted by replacing the original drugs with their generic counterparts and negotiating prices for the reimbursed drugs. Efficiency may also be enhanced by reducing reliance on hospital care. This can be done through the better use of hospital beds and outpatient contacts, as well as by reducing the number of beds [22–24].

S. Mirmirani, H. Li and A. Ilacqua compared the efficiency of health systems in eight selected post-Soviet countries with average results for the OECD countries. The study was conducted for the years 1997–2001. The inputs used included per capita health-care expenditure in USD, PPP, number of inpatient hospital beds per thousand population, number of physicians per thousand population and the percentage of children with measles inoculation. The "immunization" is used as a proxy variable. The average life expectancy of both sexes at birth and infant mortality rates is used as output variables [18].

4. The proposed model and the utilized data

The data envelopment analysis (DEA) non-parametric method of measuring the relative efficiency has been developed rapidly since 1978, when a novel article "Measuring the efficiency of decision making units" by A. Charnes, W.W. Cooper and E. Rhodes was published [25]. DEA is a data-oriented approach to the evaluation of functioning of a set of peer entities called decision-making units (DMUs), which transform multiple inputs to multiple outputs

[26]. The definition of DMU is rather general to provide the flexibility to use it in a wide range of possible applications. DMU is generally regarded as an object responsible for converting inputs to outputs, the action of which is to be evaluated [27], which allows for the use of this method in many different contexts, both in manufacturing and in almost all public sectors.

The usefulness of the method stems from the possibility of assessing the relative efficiency of decision-making units. It is used in the banking sector, health care, agriculture, transport or education for reasons that can be characterized as identifying sources of inefficiency, creating DMU rankings, evaluation of management systems, assessment of the effectiveness of programmes or policies, creating a quantitative basis for the reallocation of resources, etc. [28]. The DEA method is used in testing the efficiency of health-care systems at practically all levels, ranging from physicians (both primary and specialist care), through providers of medical services (hospitals, emergency assistance, etc.), to global, country-level assessments.

Two basic radial models, CCR (with constant returns to scale) and BCC (with variable returns to scale), evaluate the radial (proportional) efficiency but do not account for the surpluses of inputs and shortages of outputs, thus allowing for detecting only the radial inefficiencies. According to the DEA definition of efficiency, the operation of DMU is fully (100%) efficient if and only if both the efficiency score equals one and the inputs and output slacks are zero. In the case where the efficiency score is equal to one and one or both slacks are different from zero, it can be said that DMU is weakly efficient [27, 29]. This is a drawback, as the efficiency result does not take into account the non-zero slacks. This drawback is not present in the additive model, which directly takes into account the slacks in the calculation of efficiency and can distinguish between efficient and inefficient DMUs—there is, however, no possibility to measure the size of inefficiency with a scalar measure similar to that used in the basic radial models. Drawing upon the additive model, a measure of the efficiency based on slacks was developed (slack-based measure, SBM). This measure takes into account the non-zero slacks of inputs and outputs, if they are present [27]. The DEA models can be focused on the inputs or outputs, depending on which variables the decision-maker can control.

The calculations are based on the input-oriented slack-based model (SBM) under constant returns-to-scale assumption [30]. Since only the inputs are controllable by the decision-makers shaping the health policy, an input-oriented model was adopted. In an input orientation, improvement of efficiency is possible through reduction of inputs. The SBM input efficiency score ρ_I^* of DMU_o $(o = 1, \ldots, n)$ is calculated for given amounts of outputs y_{rj}, $r = 1, \ldots, s$ and inputs y_{ij}, $i = 1, \ldots, m$, where $j = 1, \ldots, n$ [26].

$$\rho_I^* = \min_{\lambda, s^-, s^+} 1 - \frac{1}{m} \sum_{i=1}^{m} \frac{s_i^-}{x_{io}} \tag{1}$$

subject to

$$x_{io} = \sum_{j=1}^{n} x_{ij} \lambda_j + s_i^- \quad (i = 1, \ldots, m) \tag{2}$$

$$y_{ro} = \sum_{j=1}^{n} y_{rj} \lambda_j - s_r^+ \quad (r = 1, \ldots, s) \tag{3}$$

$$\lambda_j \geq 0\ (\forall j), \quad s_i^- \geq 0\ (\forall i), \quad s_r^+ \geq 0\ (\forall r) \tag{4}$$

where $\boldsymbol{\lambda}$ is the intensity vector and $\mathbf{s}^-$, $\mathbf{s}^+$ are input and output slack vectors respectively.

The aim of the study is to compare the health outcomes in selected countries. The statistical information available in the case of post-communist countries is much more limited than e.g. in the case of OECD or European Union countries. The possibility of using variables in a model is determined by the consistency of measurement for post-communist countries and the availability of the data [15]. Thus, the model used three variables treated as inputs, characterizing the structure of spending and the level of income inequality. The PR_TE variable defines the share of private expenditure in total health expenditure. The OOP_TE variable determines what is the total share of the out of pocket payment in the total health expenditure. It is assumed that the lower is the public's load of private health expenditure, the higher is the availability of medical services and thus the higher is the possibility of obtaining better health outcomes in the population. The third variable, GINI, is the value of the Gini index. The Gini index is a measurement of the income distribution of a country's residents. This number, which ranges between 0 and 1 and is based on residents' net income, helps define the gap between the rich and the poor, with 0 representing perfect equality and 1 representing perfect inequality. In this model it is expressed as a percentage.

The overall health status of population is generally operationalized by indicators of longevity such as life expectancy or healthy life expectancy. So the outputs in this model are reflected by two variables: LE60—life expectancy at age 60 and HLE—healthy life expectancy at birth. The third output variable is ISR—infant survival rate, which is the opposite of infant mortality rate (IMR is unwanted output and was included in the model as the difference 1000-IMR).

Using the above-described model, the 28 post-communist countries[1] and the virtual unit (DMU) as an aggregate of average values for 16 developed countries of Western Europe[2] (DE16), which achieve very good health outcomes, were analysed. The virtual unit (DE16) consists of countries where the health system is organized according to Beveridge and Bismarck models. Data from the years 2000 and 2013 from the WHO database and The World Bank databases were used. In the case of missing data, the principle of using the nearest value was applied.

The calculations were carried out by means of the DEA-Solver-LV (3) software by Saitech.

The basic descriptive statistics of variables for years 2000 and 2013 are presented (**Table 1**).

The last row shows the difference between the mean values of the variables (2013–2000). The average share of private spending did not change; however, the share of patients' out-of-pocket payment in the total expenditure decreased by 1.0 percentage point, which is a proof of weak development of the pre-paid health insurance. The income inequalities in the countries surveyed decreased slightly, by 0.5 p.p.; however, the span of this variable increased. All results improved: LE60 increased by about 9% and HLE by 6%. The infant mortality decreased significantly: in the year 2000, it was highest in Tajikistan and amounted to 74.7 infants per

[1]Albania, Armenia, Azerbaijan, Belarus, Bosnia and Herzegovina, Bulgaria, Croatia, Czech Republic, Estonia, Georgia, Hungary, Kazakhstan, Kyrgyzstan, Latvia, Lithuania, Montenegro, Poland, Republic of Macedonia, Republic of Moldova, Romania, Russian Federation, Serbia, Slovakia, Slovenia, Tajikistan, Turkmenistan Ukraine, Uzbekistan.

[2]Austria, Belgium, Denmark, Finland, France, Germany, Iceland, Ireland, Italy, Luxembourg, Netherlands, Norway, Spain, Sweden, Switzerland and United Kingdom.

Year	Statistics	PR_TE	OOP_TE	GINI	LE60	HLE	IMR
2000	Mean	41.2	37.8	32.8	17.9	62.6	23.3
	Stand. error	21.3	20.9	3.6	1.1	2.9	19.1
	Max	83.0	82.5	40.8	20.4	66.8	74.7
	Min	9.7	9.7	27.2	15.7	56.6	4.5
2013	Mean	41.2	36.8	32.3	19.5	66.3	12.3
	Stand. error	15.9	14.9	5.1	1.5	2.6	11.8
	Max	79.2	71.1	44.1	23.4	71.1	46.6
	Min	16.7	12.1	24.7	16.4	59.8	2.3
Mean 2013 – mean 2000		0.0	–1.0	–0.5	1.6	3.7	–11.0

Source: Own computation.

Table 1. The basic descriptive statistics of variables for years 2000 and 2013.

1000 live births. In 2013, the highest infant mortality rate was reported in Turkmenistan—46.6 infants per 1000 live births. In 2000, it was 17 times higher and in 2013, 20 times higher than the lowest mortality observed in these years in Slovenia.

5. The results and their interpretation

The results of computation are shown (**Table 2**).

Column "Score" contains the efficiency score and column "R" the position in the ranking. In the year 2000, the full efficiency (score equal to 1.000) was achieved by the Czech Republic, Hungary, Slovenia and the virtual DMU referred to as DE16, which were among the best also in 2013 (besides Hungary). The full efficiency in 2013 was also reached by Croatia and Ukraine.

In 2013, six countries reduced their efficiency score—in the case of two of them, it was significant. Hungary, with full efficiency in 2000, achieved the level of only 0.627 in 2013, and Slovakia achieved a result of 0.753 in 2013, compared to 0.923 in the year 2000. The other four countries lowered their efficiency score to a negligible degree.

On the other hand, the remaining countries improved their scores, of which 7 to significant degree (above 0.15). The greatest improvement was achieved by Croatia and Ukraine, which reached full efficiency, improving the result by 0.234 and 0.548 respectively. Bosnia and Herzegovina, Estonia, Kazakhstan, Kyrgyzstan and Poland improved their result by 0.15–0.23.

For a more detailed analysis of the causes of these positive and negative changes Hungary, Slovakia, Croatia, Ukraine, Azerbaijan and Georgia were selected. The table includes also additional aggregated data for the most developed economies of Western Europe—DE16, which should be considered to constitute best practice. The source data for the input and output variables for these countries for the years 2000 and 2013 are presented (**Table 3**).

Country	2000		2013		Country	2000		2013	
	Score	R	Score	R		Score	R	Score	R
Albania	0.383	22	0.508	21	Lithuania	0.518	12	0.574	15
Armenia	0.334	27	0.472	24	Macedonia	0.417	19	0.543	16
Azerbaijan	0.324	28	0.407	28	Moldova	0.382	23	0.514	20
Belarus	0.653	7	0.653	10	Montenegro	0.523	11	0.523	19
Bosnia and Herzegovina	0.454	15	0.622	12	Poland	0.496	14	0.680	9
Bulgaria	0.441	17	0.507	22	Romania	0.645	8	0.784	7
Croatia	0.766	6	1.000	1	Russian Federation	0.430	18	0.423	27
Czech Republic	1.000	1	1.000	1	Serbia	0.501	13	0.577	14
Estonia	0.561	9	0.795	6	Slovakia	0.923	5	0.753	8
Georgia	0.297	29	0.363	29	Slovenia	1.000	1	1.000	1
Hungary	1.000	1	0.627	11	Tajikistan	0.365	25	0.435	26
Kazakhstan	0.379	24	0.542	17	Turkmenistan	0.539	10	0.504	23
Kyrgyzstan	0.403	20	0.587	13	Ukraine	0.452	16	1.000	1
Latvia	0.402	21	0.533	18	Uzbekistan	0.360	26	0.458	25
					DE16	1.000	1	1.000	1

Source: Own computation.
In columns score where the result = 1 the countries have a full efficiency.

Table 2. Efficiency scores for the years 2000 and 2013.

Country	Year	PR_TE	OOP_TE	GINI	LE60	HLE	ISR
Hungary	2000	29.3	26.3	27.2	18.3	63.7	990.3
	2013	36.4	27.5	30.6	20.1	67.4	994.8
Slovakia	2000	10.6	10.6	28.9	18.3	64.9	989.8
	2013	30.0	22.1	26.1	20.3	68.1	994.0
Croatia	2000	13.9	13.9	31.3	19.3	66.4	992.8
	2013	20.0	12.5	32.5	21.2	69.4	996.2
Ukraine	2000	48.2	44.1	29.1	16.7	60.6	984.2
	2013	45.5	42.8	24.7	18.1	64.1	991.4
Azerbaijan	2000	81.4	63.3	36.5	16.8	59.3	939.3
	2013	79.2	71.1	31.8	18.5	64.7	970.1
Georgia	2000	83.0	82.5	40.5	18.6	64.1	968.8
	2013	78.5	61.9	41.4	19.7	66.4	988.3
DE_16	2000	24.0	16.7	30.9	21.9	69.0	995.5
	2013	21.9	15.3	30.5	24.1	71.9	997.1

Source: Own computation.

Table 3. Data from selected countries for the years 2000 and 2013.

The primary reason for the decrease of efficiency in Hungary and Slovakia is a very significant change in the financing structure. The PR_TE variable increased by 7.1 p.p. in Hungary and as much as 19.4 p.p. in Slovakia, whereas the OOP_TE variable increased by 1.7 p.p. in Hungary and as much as 11.5 p.p. in Slovakia. In the case of Hungary, these negative phenomena coincided with an increase in the income inequalities of the society, illustrated by the change in the GINI index from 27.2 in 2000 to 30.6 in 2013. In the case of Slovakia, the inequalities decreased. It should be noted, however, the all the health outcomes in these two countries improved.

In the case of Croatia, which improved its efficiency score, there was indeed an increase in the share of private expenditure (PR_TE) but the expenses covered directly by households (OOP_TE) decreased. The GINI index deteriorated slightly. On the other hand, in the case of Ukraine both private spending (PR_TE) and the expenditure covered directly by the public (OOP_TE) decreased. Also the income inequalities in the population (GINI) decreased significantly. The favourable results of Ukraine since 2014 deteriorated due to the ongoing military conflict.

Azerbaijan and Georgia reduced the share of private spending by 2.2 and 4.5 p.p., respectively. These expenses are about two times higher than the average for post-communist countries and almost four times higher than the average for developed countries of Western Europe. The share of direct expenditure in Azerbaijan increased by 7.8 p.p., while in Georgia it decreased by 20.6 p.p. The income inequalities fell by 4.7 percentage points in Azerbaijan and increased slightly by 0.9 p.p. in Georgia. The health outcomes improved.

http://dx.doi.org/10.5772/67817

Figure 1 is the illustration of the efficiency scores shown in **Table 3** of the changes described above. The efficiency scores are shown in descending order, which allows for the analysis of the direction and magnitude of change.

The conducted analysis allows for indicating several typical situations. The countries that achieved better health outcomes are those in which there is a low level of private spending, such as e.g. the Czech Republic (16.7%). The higher share of private spending is seen in Croatia and Slovenia, but these countries have low share of out-of-pocket expenses—62.4% and 42.7% respectively. These are the only two post-communist countries in which the voluntary private insurances operate effectively. Increasing the share of private spending while increasing direct expenditure affected the health results achieved by Hungary and Slovakia negatively. A very high share of private expenditure and at the same time a high share out of pocket payments contributes to the achievement of worse health outcomes.

The share of private expenditure in the total expenditure (PR_TE) on healthcare and the share of patients' out-of-pocket payments (OOP_TE) are the variables which indirectly characterize the barriers in access to healthcare services. Of course, the obtained results should not be interpreted as meaning that a change in the financing structure has a direct impact on the improvement of health outcomes. However, the indirect effect has been demonstrated, which confirms the results of other authors dealing with research on the availability of medical services for patients.

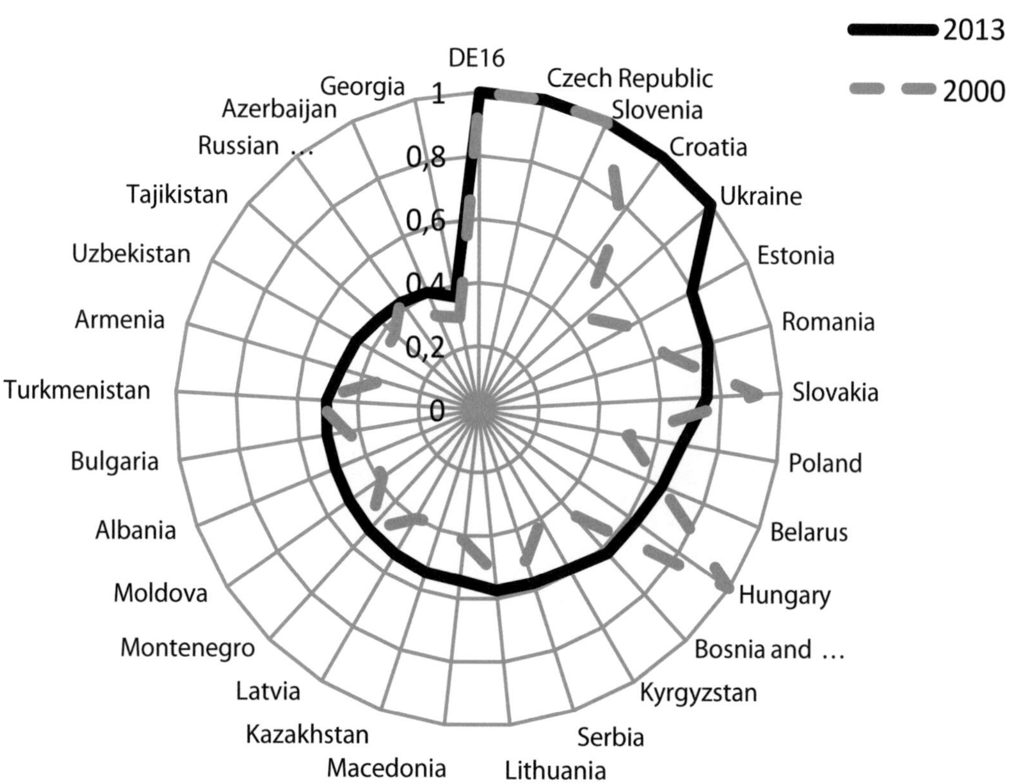

Figure 1. Comparison of the effectiveness results in the years 2000 and 2013. Source: Own elaboration.

The next step of the analysis is to provide a projection, that is the directions and magnitudes of changes that should be introduced by the inefficient countries in order to achieve the efficiency of leaders. This is illustrated in **Table 4**. The calculations were carried out for the year 2013.

Country	PR_TE		OOP_TE		GINI	
	Data	Change	Data	Change	Data	Change
Albania	51.6	−0.678	51.5	−0.697	29.0	−0.102
Armenia	58.3	−0.717	54.7	−0.716	30.5	−0.152
Azerbaijan	58.3	−0.795	54.7	−0.785	30.5	−0.200
Belarus	34.6	−0.518	31.9	−0.508	26.5	−0.016
Bosnia and Herzegovina	30.0	−0.445	29.0	−0.460	33.8	−0.230
Bulgaria	40.7	−0.593	39.6	−0.606	36.0	−0.280
Estonia	22.1	−0.241	18.9	−0.165	33.2	−0.208
Georgia	78.5	−0.789	61.9	−0.748	41.35	−0.374
Hungary	36.4	−0.542	27.5	−0.430	30.6	−0.147
Kazakhstan	46.9	−0.648	46.3	−0.665	27.5	−0.060
Kyrgyzstan	41.0	−0.600	36.4	−0.577	27.4	−0.063
Latvia	38.1	−0.564	36.5	−0.572	35.5	−0.267
Lithuania	33.4	−0.501	32.6	−0.519	35.2	−0.257
Macedonia	31.1	−0.465	31.1	−0.497	44.05	−0.409
Moldova	54.0	−0.694	44.6	−0.652	29.2	−0.113
Montenegro	42.7	−0.610	42.7	−0.633	32.2	−0.190
Poland	30.4	−0.452	22.8	−0.313	32.4	−0.195
Romania	20.3	−0.184	19.7	−0.209	34.9	−0.257
Russian Federation	51.9	−0.680	48.0	−0.675	41.6	−0.375
Serbia	39.5	−0.578	37.9	−0.587	29.1	−0.103
Slovakia	30.0	−0.445	22.1	−0.292	26.1	−0.003
Tajikistan	69.4	−0.769	60.1	−0.749	30.5	−0.177
Turkmenistan	34.5	−0.537	34.5	−0.565	40.8	−0.387
Uzbekistan	45.5	−0.671	42.8	−0.671	24.7	−0.284

Source: Own computation.

Table 4. Projection of changes in the inefficient countries for the year 2013.

The DATA columns contain the values of the respective variables registered in 2013. The CHANGE columns present the percentage change, the introduction of which would lead to achieving full efficiency in individual countries. The direction of these changes is the same for all variables and countries, and the size varies. The changes are for PR_TE from 0.184 to 0.795, for OOP_TE from 0.165 to 0.785 and for GINI from 0.003 to 0.409.

In order to achieve full efficiency, these countries should change the structure of financing and income inequalities, e.g. Azerbaijan should reduce PR_TE by 79.5%, OOP_TE by 78.5% and GINI by 20.0%, whereas Georgia should reduce PR_TE by 78.9%, OOP_TE by 74.8% and GINI by 37.4%, which to reduce the proportion of people at risk of catastrophic health expenditures in this countries [31].

6. Conclusion

The health care systems of the post-communist countries are financed according to the historical burden of the past: the Central Europe is dominated by funding with health insurance contributions, while in Eastern Europe and Central Asia the budgetary financing prevails. Financing health care from health insurance premiums appears to be more stable than budget financing, although it is also vulnerable to economic fluctuations. However, as in the Western European countries, the health insurance system should be supplemented with budget funds. The problem of the former Eastern bloc countries is the low amounts that may be used to finance health care services, medications, rehabilitation or additional services. The costs of medical equipment and medicines are similar in all the countries, and in many of them, only basic treatments and therapies with generic drugs instead of original (modern) ones are financed. Thus, in many countries, there are difficulties in access to modern medical technologies.

Limiting the extensive infrastructure of the health care sector and the financing of the health needs of the population, as opposed to facilities, is the key to improving the performance of health systems. An unsolved problem related to the efficiency and financing is low salaries of medical staff in the surveyed countries.

The study of health systems efficiency in 28 post-communist countries indicates significant differences between the compared countries (DMUs). As a target and, at the same time, the basis for comparison, the aggregated health system of the 16 developed countries of Western Europe, which achieves very good health outcomes (DE16), was indicated. Comparable health outcomes are also achieved by three most developed countries of Central and Eastern Europe: Slovenia, Czech Republic and Croatia. In Croatia, the infant mortality rate is currently slightly higher than in the case of the other leaders.

It is postulated that in all the countries a system of co-payments for the use of health care, understood as the cost of access to the health care system, should be introduced. The aim of such action would be to rationalize demand. It could also reduce the scale of informal fees and slightly raise the total funding of the system. It is also postulated that the countries of

Central Asia should increase public funding in order to provide citizens with access to health care (e.g. Kyrgyzstan).

It is also necessary to determine the exact package of benefits—health services which will be financed from public funds. This would allow for the development of voluntary health insurance, from which above-standard services would be funded.

It is imperative to strengthen the role of the general practitioner and ambulatory health care, as well as reduce the number of inpatients. In many countries, doctors working as general practitioners have rather low qualifications and the raising their qualifications is necessary [32].

The instability of employment, lack of social protection, low wages, income inequalities and psychological stress additionally contribute to high number of suicides, large number of civilization-related disease cases, and as a result, shorter life expectancy. In transition countries, the life expectancy is on average 8 years shorter than in Western Europe, while healthy life expectancy is 7 years shorter.

The problem of excessive alcohol consumption in some post-Soviet countries and the high percentage of tobacco consumers remains unresolved. Another problem is the unhealthy lifestyle, poor nutrition, inactivity and a high percentage of overweight people. The post-socialist way of thinking and the low performance of health care systems combined with low financing are the causes of poor health care outcomes.

Author details

Justyna Kujawska

Address all correspondence to: Justyna.Kujawska@zie.pg.gda.pl

Gdansk University of Technology, Gdansk, Poland

References

[1] González E., Cárcaba A., Ventura J. Value efficiency analysis of health systems: does public financing play a role? Journal of Public Health. 2010;**18**(4):337-350. DOI: 10.1007/s10389-009-0311-4

[2] Kumar A., Ozdamar L., Ng C.P. Procurement performance measurement system in the health care industry. International Journal of Health Care Quality Assurance. 2005; **18**(2):152-166. DOI: 10.1108/09526860510588179

[3] Anell A., Willis M. International comparison of health care systems using resource profiles. Bulletin of the World Health Organization. 2000;**78**(6):770-778.

[4] de Cos P.H., Moral-Benito E. Determinants of health-system efficiency: evidence from OECD countries. International Journal of Health Care Finance and Economics. 2014;**14**(1):69-93. DOI: 10.1007/s10754-013-9140-7

[5] Rowland D., Telyukov A.V. Soviet health care from two perspectives. Health Affairs. 1991;**10**(3):71-86. DOI: 10.1377/hlthaff.10.3.71

[6] Wagstaff A., van Doorslaer E., Calonge S., Christiansen T., Gerfin M., Gottschalk P., et al. Equity in the finance of health care: some international comparisons. Journal of Health Economics. 1992;**11**(4):361-387.

[7] OECD/EU. Health at a Glance 2016: Europe 2016 – State of Health in the EU Cycle. 1st ed. Paris: OECD Publishing; 2015. 199 p. DOI: 10.1787/9789264265592-en

[8] Wendt C. Changing healthcare system types. Social Policy & Administration. 2014; **48**(7):864-882. DOI: 10.1111/spol.12061

[9] Xu K., Evans D.B., Carrin G., Aguilar-Rivera A.M. Designing health financing systems to reduce catastrophic health expenditure. Technical Brief for Policy-Makers WHO. 2005;**2**:1-4.

[10] Xu K., Evans D.B., Kawabata K., Zeramdini R., Klavus J., Murray C.J.L. Household catastrophic health expenditure: a multicountry analysis. Lancet. 2003;**362**(9378):111-117. DOI: 10.1016/S0140-6736(03)13861-5

[11] Xu K., Evans D.B., Carrin G., Aguilar-Rivera A.M., Musgrove P., Evans T. Protecting households from catastrophic health spending. Health Affairs. 2007;**26**(4):972-983. DOI: 10.1377/hlthaff.26.4.972

[12] Kujawska J. Konkurencja między płatnikami a skuteczność działania systemów ochrony zdrowia nowych państw członkowskch Unii Europejskiej. In: Grynia A., editor. Czynniki organiczające oraz poprawiające konkurencyjność nowych krajów członkowskich Unii Europejskiej. 1st ed. Vilnus: Uniwersytet w Białymstoku; 2016. pp. 314-328.

[13] Kutzin J., Ibraimova A., Jakab M., O'Dougherty S. Bismarck meets Beveridge on the Silk Road: coordinating funding sources to create a universal health financing system in Kyrgyzstan. Bulletin World Health Organization. 2009;**87**(7):549-554. DOI: 10.2471/BLT.07.049544

[14] McKee M., Healy J., Falkingham J., editors. Health Care in Central Asia. 1st ed. Buckingham, Philadelphia: Open University Press; 2002. 222 p.

[15] Rechel B., Richardson E., McKee M., editors. Trends in Health Systems in the Former Soviet Countries. 1st ed. Copenhagen: European Observatory on Health Systems and Policies; 2014. 227 p.

[16] Retzlaff-Roberts D., Chang C.F., Rubin R.M. Technical efficiency in the use of health care resources: a comparison of OECD countries. Health Policy. 2004;**69**(1):55-72. DOI: 10.1016/j.healthpol.2003.12.002

[17] Afonso A., Aubyn M.ST. Non-parametric approaches to education and health efficiency in OECD countries. Journal of Applied Economics. 2005;**VIII**(2):227-246.

[18] Mirmirani S., Li H.C., Ilacqua J.A. Health care efficiency in transition economies: an application of Data Envelopment Analysis. International Business & Economics Research Journal. 2008;**7**(2):47-54. DOI: 10.19030/iber.v7i2.3221

[19] Hadad S., Hadad Y., Simon-Tuval T. Determinants of healthcare system#x2019;s efficiency in OECD countries. European Journal of Health Economics. 2013;**14**(2):253-265. DOI: 10.1007/s10198-011-0366-3

[20] Papanicolas I., Smith P.C., editors. Health System Performance Comparison. An Agenda for Policy, Information and Research. 1st ed. New York: Open University Press; 2013. 384 p.

[21] Or Z., Wang J., Jamison D. International differences in the impact of doctors on health: a multilevel analysis of OECD countries. Journal of Health Economics. 2005;**24**(3):531-560. DOI: 10.1016/j.jhealeco.2004.09.003

[22] Verhoeven M., Gunnarsson V., Lugaresi S. The Health Sector in the Slovak Republic: Efficiency and Reform. IMF Working Paper, WP/07/226. 1st ed. Washington: International Monetary Fund; 2007. 25 p.

[23] Jafarov E., Gunnarsson V. Government Spending on Health Care and Education in Croatia: Efficiency and Reform Options. IMF Working Paper, WP/08/136. 1st ed. Washington: International Monetary Fund; 2008. 34 p.

[24] Grigoli F. Public Expenditure in the Slovak Republic: Composition and Technical Efficiency. IMF Working Paper, WP/12/173. 1st ed. Washington: International Monetary Fund; 2012. 33 p.

[25] Charnes A., Cooper W.W., Rhodes E. Measuring the efficiency of decision making units. European Journal of Operational Research. 1978;**6**:429-444. DOI: 10.1016/0377-2217(78)90138-8

[26] Cooper W.W., Seiford L.M., Zhu J., editors. Handbook on Data Envelopment Analysis. New York, Dordrecht, Heidelberg, London: Springer; 2011. 497 p. DOI: 10.1007/978-1-4419-6151-8

[27] Cooper W.W., Seiford L.M., Tone K. Data Envelopment Analysis. A Comprehensive Text with Models, Applications, References and DEA Solver Software. 1st ed. Boston/Dordrecht/London: Kluwer Academic Publishers; 2000. 318 p. DOI: 10.1007/b109347

[28] Liu J.S., Lu L.Y.Y., Lu W.M., Lin B.J.Y. A survey of DEA applications. Omega. 2013;**41**(5):893-902. DOI: 10.1016/j.omega.2012.11.004

[29] Zhu J., Cook W.D., editors. Modelling Data Irregularities and Structural Complexities in Data Envelopment Analysis. 1st ed. New York: Springer; 2007. 333 p. DOI: 10.1007/978-0-387-71607-7

[30] Hsu Y.C. Efficiency in government health spending: a super slacks-based model. Quality and Quantity. 2014;**48**(1):111-126. DOI: 10.1007/s11135-012-9753-9

[31] Gotsadze G., Zoidze A., Rukhadze N. Household catastrophic health expenditure: evidence from Georgia and its policy implications. BMC Health Services Research. 2009;**9**(69):1-9. DOI: 10.1186/1472-6963-9-69

[32] Rechel B., McKee M. Health reform in central and eastern Europe and the former Soviet Union. Lancet. 2009;**374**(3 Oct):1186-1195. DOI: 10.1016/S0140-6736(09)61334-9

Chapter 7

Health Support in the Palm of Your Hand: The Role of Technology in Achieving Health Goals

Alicia De la Pena and Bernardo Amezcua

Additional information is available at the end of the chapter

http://dx.doi.org/10.5772/67768

Abstract

Smartphones have transformed how individuals engage with each other, their leisure time, their work, and even the way they take care of their health. With a qualitative study, we explore how Smartphone apps and social network sites (SNSs) are being used by individuals who want to take care of their health. Findings suggest that individuals are taking advantage of digital technologies to improve their wellbeing in several manners: they use wearable devices to monitor their health and track their physical activity, keep in touch with doctors and health coaches using instant mobile messaging applications, and join virtual communities seeking for advice and support. Being a member of these communities provides certain advantages and rewards that motivate individuals to act on their good intentions toward their health. Given the high rates of adoption of digital technologies, specific social marketing campaigns can be designed to influence health behavior, including health promotion and interventions to help individuals achieve personal goals and improve the quality of their life.

Keywords: behavioral economics, health goals, mHealth, smartphones, social support, social networks

1. Introduction

Individuals set health-related goals all the time. While some of them want to quit smoking, others are seeking to run a half marathon, lose some pounds, or keep their diabetes in check. According to the theory of planned behavior [1], individuals have all the necessary resources, skills, and abilities to perform the behavior at will. However, successful behavior change does not happen at once. For some, a little nudge is needed to encourage them to take the required steps to attain a health-related goal [2]. Technology, and specifically Smartphone Apps and wearable devices can provide the incentives, feedback, and information individuals need to take their health into their own hands and improve their wellbeing. At the same time, social support can also become a tool to help those individuals who are willing to change their unhealthy behaviors, but need some encouragement and instrumental assistance to reach their health goals [3], such support can be provided face-to-face, or with the use of digital technology that allows individuals to gather in social network sites (SNSs) to seek and receive health advice and encouragement.

To gain a deeper understanding on how individuals use technology and social network sites to improve their health, a qualitative study was conducted in three stages. Phase 1 includes a netnography on two health-related Facebook communities conducted for a six-month period. In the second phase, in-depth interviews were conducted with five bariatric surgery patients. As part of their recovery, they created a Whatasapp and a Telegram group to receive encouragement and provide tips to keep the weight off and eat balanced meals. In the third phase, in-depth interviews were conducted with individuals who use their Smartphones as tools to monitor their health-related activities. All in-depth interviews were recorded, transcribed, and analyzed; for the netnography online, data were captured in text files using word-processing software, photos, and the other images published by SNS users were captured as screen shots of the computer screen as they appeared online [4, 5]. Then we conducted a content analysis that allowed us to gain a better understanding of how individuals make use of digital technologies to take care of their health issues.

In this chapter, we seek to present our findings and illustrate on the use of technology as a tool to increase health and wellbeing. In the first part, we explore key concepts regarding the use of digital technologies and present some theoretical bases of social support and behavioral economics; finally, we describe the findings of our qualitative study to illustrate how individuals are using the Internet and digital technologies to improve their lifestyle.

2. Digital technologies and mHealth

Most individuals cannot imagine leaving home without their mobile phones. Nearly all adults in the US now have cellphones [6] and half of those are smartphones. In countries such as Australia, Italy, China, the United Kingdom, and South Korea, smartphone penetration reaches almost 70% of the adult population [7], while the adoption rate of smartphones is less than 30% in places such as Mexico (20%), Egypt (26%), Argentina (24%), and Brazil (14%) [8].

As smartphones and tables provide consumers with more access to content and multimedia features, consumers' habits are being transformed around the world. Such devices are being used to play games, shop, connect with social networks, and even for taking care of health issues. In fact, Smartphones and other ubiquitous technologies can be the solution in providing consolidated information in an understandable and meaningful form that will actually help people to make better choices [9].

Nowadays, individuals are demonstrating an active interest in health issues and moving from being patients to being consumers of a vast variety of health products and health services. Of those, a good number (67%) are interested in using online technologies and new media to improve their health and wellbeing [10]. Interest is also high in using a device to monitor fitness and wellness goals as well as for managing specific health conditions, like diabetes. As many as 41% of consumers are interested in using an app to set goals and monitor their progress as well as get gentle reminders that they need to get up and begin their exercise routine, and 38% of smartphone users consider their device as an essential tool for finding health and medical information [11, 12].

With the widespread use of mobile technologies to support the achievement of health goals objectives, the World Health Organization has come with a new term: mHealth; to refer to the health practice supported by mobile devices and its applications. mHealth apps can be divided into two categories: health and fitness apps (e.g., MyFitnessPal, MyNetDiary, LoseIt) that help consumers monitor their healthy activities; and apps that pair with wearable devices and transmit data to a dashboard (e.g., Nike Fuel Band, FitBit, Apple iWatch, BellaBeat). The data can be used both by health care providers and patients to view trends, patient events (e.g., an asthma attack), and adherence to specific programs (e.g., use of medication). Usually, the apps provide users with weekly reports summarizing their experience and programs and providing educational content and interventions to help them achieve their health-related goals [12, 13]. For those consumers seeking to improve their health, digital technologies and the Internet provide three major benefits: immediate access to information, health-tracking tools, and virtual communities for support [14].

Even though the dashboard by itself is useful for providing specific data for the user (e.g., number of miles walked or amount of calories consumed), the feedback provided can help individuals to adhere to new health-related habits if it is designed using concepts of behavioral economics, which implies the use of challenges, rewards, social norms, and visual elements, among other features to motivate individuals to adhere to a new routine or lifestyle [15]. At the same time, previous research suggests that digital technology will provide better results if it is combined with social encouragement and collaboration from peers facing a similar situation [16], therefore, the importance on learning about social support.

3. Social support

Social support groups have been present for many decades. It was in the early 1980s when a new social movement conformed by individuals seeking for social support to alleviate or mitigate the effects of their overconsumption patterns (e.g., Alcoholics Anonymous, Overeaters Anonymous) emerged [17]. Support groups are voluntary affiliations, formed by peers who rely on the expertise and testimonials of members, who provide each other with mutual assistance, feedback, and methods to deal with their problems [18].

And event though, social support groups began with gatherings in church basements and school meeting rooms, they have moved to SNS, where there is no fixed schedule for the meetings, physical contact, or face-to-face interactions full of embarrassment for confessing in the middle of a circle of peers one more missed section at the gym, or devouring a big bowl of ice cream each night [19]. Nowadays, encounters take place online, using the advances of digital technology like Facebook groups, which allow meeting peers who share similar values and goals, and who have joined the digital communities to receive the much-needed social support.

Individuals who use online communities can chat on the website, write about their health-related problems, and support each other with specific advice. In certain communities, members can update their health information and receive tailored suggestions, such as daily calorie intake and customized exercise plans, as well as motivational messages from their friends to help them adhere to their goals, or receive encouragement when they are ready to re-start their exercise routine after a relapse; with the advantage of remaining anonymous or using nicknames that will protect them from embarrassing moments and hard critics [20, 21].

One of the advantages of online communities is that they are customized for specific needs. Usually, they are characterized according to the activity they provide (e.g., social support, health advice), the people whom they serve (e.g., breast cancer survivors), or the technology that supports them (e.g., linked to a wearable device). In these communities, individuals can find and provide four types of support: (1) emotional (e.g., friendship, trust, empathy); (2) instrumental (tangible aid); (3) informational (e.g., advice or suggestions); and (4) constructive feedback; which in sum become a form of social capital of high value for individuals [3].

Even though, SNSs allow different types of interactions and relationships, what distinguishes social support from other interactions are some specific characteristics: social support is always intended to be helpful, is consciously provided in an interpersonal context of caring and respect, and in the case of informational support, it can attempt to influence the behaviors and decisions of the receiver [3].

4. How individuals make decisions

According to standard economic theory, individuals are fully rational when making decisions, they try to maximize utility and when given information, they are able to make optimal decisions. But behavioral economics (BE) suggests otherwise: consumer behavior is complex, people sometimes make irrational choices, and their behavior does not follow the predictions of economic models. Most people are risk averse and prefer to make decisions based on heuristics or mental shortcuts to reduce efforts and avoid hassles [22]. They also are motivated by rewards and respond easily to incentives and nudges. A nudge is any factor that significantly alters people's behavior in a predictable way. The nudge can be designed by a choice architect, who has the responsibility for organizing the context in which people makes decisions. The nudge can be as simple as the use of specific colors. Most drivers know that they have to stop when they see a red light, and keep driving their cars if the light turns to green. This common knowledge —and way of nudging—has then moved to another areas of people's life, for example, with the use of traffic lights, food labels, and graphics to indicate the energy consumption in the household, social marketers attempt to design and use easy to understand tools to educate and orientate consumers and help them in making wise choices [2].

Besides the nudges, a good way to help individuals to improve their performance is to provide them with prompt and specific feedback, that will help them learn when they are doing well and when they are making mistakes or moving away from their goals. Feedback can assist individuals in monitoring their health-related goals and help them form new habits and internalize specific behaviors. Feedback that includes action steps to achieve a goal or provide comparative information is considered more useful for people. At the same time, a good choice architect needs to provide the right incentives or rewards in order to motivate individuals to maintain the desired behavior. Finally, people also tend to measure their performance and wellbeing in relative terms, by comparing with others in similar situations and trying to comply with social norms that reflect the behaviors and attitudes commonly accepted by a social group [2, 23].

5. Application

In their quest for health and wellbeing, people are turning to technology to reach and maintain their health-related goals and improve their lifestyle. It seems that nowadays, the Internet, the Smartphones, and even jewelry and clothing apparel play an important role in managing specific health conditions. In this section, we describe how digital platforms and technology provide advantages to individuals who need support to reach and maintain their health goals. First, we illustrate how SNS have become commonplace for individuals who seek physical wellbeing and address their need for social support. Second, we describe how patients are using mobile messaging applications to receive instrumental and informational support. And third, we explore the motives to use wearable devices and health monitoring apps.

5.1. Facebook communities

Worldwide there are over 1.79 billion people using Facebook each month. On average, each individual spends around 20 minutes in each visit, and almost 93% of Facebook users reach the SNS from their mobile phones. With more than 650 million of groups available on Facebook, nowadays, individuals have a vast offer of communities where they can meet with virtual friends who share common interests and causes [24]. Online support groups like Weight Watchers, Alcoholic Anonymous, and numerous others provide an adequate environment for voluntary affiliations and facilitate the pursuit of wellbeing with different tools and features that allow individuals to share their fears, doubts, and struggles while trying to achieve a healthier lifestyle.

5.1.1. The method

To shed more light on how individuals are using SNS to provide and receive the four types of support, we conducted a participant netnography in two different Facebook communities. The first one related with dieting (Weight Watchers), and the second one regarding physical activity (Rapport Runners). The selected communities are highly interactive, heterogeneous, and provide rich data for analysis, as suggested by experts on this qualitative methodology [4]. Members of the two communities are active, constantly posting questions and answers, as well as uploading photos and videos.

To begin the netnography, one of the authors became a participant-observer, interacting as full participant in the local culture, contributing with comments and receiving feedback, always ensuring the ethical treatment of the data posted by the members of the community [4]. The unit of analysis consisted of two random discussion threads containing one initial post by a support seeker and several subsequent response posts published by support providers. As the study evolved, we selected other discussion threads. Online data were captured using word-processing software for further content analysis, and photos and other images were captured as visual images to be also analyzed. A qualitative content analysis was then conducted to identify potential themes, form categories, and classify participants into different segments.

5.1.2. *The findings*

The content analysis reveals that the SNSs under study offer a virtual community, where individuals can find encouragement, answers to specific health-related questions, and applause from virtual friends who cheer them up when they attain their goals. Members of the community were classified into two main categories: support providers and support seekers. Each category was then divided into subcategories based on specific traits and characteristics of participants.

Support providers were subclassified into three categories: (1) experts (e.g., doctor, health coach, nutritionist); (2) ordinary members of the community (i.e., virtual friends and acquaintances); and (3) opportunistic (i.e., individuals offering different products for sale, such as vitamins, diet pills).

While support seekers were divided into six categories: (1) anxious and fearful (i.e., individuals afraid of diseases); (2) careless and free (i.e., those individuals who expressed interest for feeling good, avoid stress, and have fun); (3) body conscious (i.e., centered in their looks and physical appearance); (4) techies (i.e., individuals who use specific apps to monitor their health and physical activity, and post their achievements in the SNS); (5) eternal dieters (i.e., individuals who seem to be stuck in their weight loss program and express their failures online); and (6) the window shoppers: the passive individuals that barely post any question or comment but take advantage of the "Like" feature of Facebook. They benefit by reading the posts published by other members of the community and show their interest and agreement by "Liking" those comments that are meaningful for them.

In the majority of posts, the initial conversation was phrased as a question or as a request for advice. Participants usually referred to the difficulty to stick to their goals (e.g., "I want to eat healthy, but I do not like vegetables, do you have any healthy recipes."); their lack of knowledge regarding a health issue (e.g., "Can I reverse my diabetes if I lose some weight?"), or their fears (e.g., "Will I hurt my knees if I start running? I am really overweight.").

http://dx.doi.org/10.5772/67768

Given that the SNSs studied have a specific target, the online environment makes it easier for participants to receive advice and encouragement from peers who are going through similar experiences, providing a frame of trust and empathy for most members of the community. While the presence of experts allows for the provision of reliable information, the advice becomes more meaningful and the support seeker feels listened to and appreciated.

In both the communities, we found the four basic forms of social support and an additional one that we called "network support." Informational support was provided when answering questions with new facts and suggesting recipes for cooking healthy food; emotional support and constructive feedback were demonstrated with messages of encouragement and emoticons showing smiley faces, clapping hands, and thumbs up icons; while tangible assistance was provided by recommending apps, diets, pills, or running shoes, among other products. Finally, the network support is an inherent characteristic of the both communities. When people join the virtual community, they get access to new people facing similar situations or similar goals, who are able to listen with more empathy and to provide specific advice.

We observed a sense of connectedness among the members of the communities, who provide psychological gratification, help individuals to release stress and guilty feelings, and in sum achieve higher levels of wellbeing. In both the cases, the studied communities offer the best of two worlds: the virtual and the face-to-face interactions. Even though we studied the online communities by reading the posts, we learned that both Weight Watchers and Rapport offer their members the opportunity to interact in face-to-face encounters. In fact, Weight Watchers was born in 1963 as a traditional support group for people willing to lose weight, and moved to Facebook just recently to take advantage of the digital technologies and provide different tools for members of the community. While Rapport was created in 2009, people achieved physical and mental goals using neurolinguistic programming and physical activity training. Members of the Rapport community meet weekly for physical training and share questions, photos, and other messages on Facebook.

Members of the studied communities are motivated by common interests and goals. They present certain levels of altruism by offering specific advice and nutritional tips to other members of the community. By choosing when and what to post, members of the virtual communities receive the support when they fail to reach their health-related goals, and the appraisal and recognition for their achievements. At the same time, we identified the presence of social trust. Individuals disclose personal topics, like the low self-esteem derived from being overweight, the struggle to find nice clothes to wear to be physically attractive, and even the criticism they receive from friends and family for not being able to achieve their health-related goals.

5.2. Nudging people toward a better lifestyle with Telegram and Whatsapp

Bariatric surgery has become an option for adults who need to lose weight for medical reasons. Among other benefits, the surgery reduces the incidence of diabetes and hypertension, but in order to be effective, patients need to make important changes in their eating habits and exercise behaviors. In sum, a new lifestyle comes in order and education, advice, and help are needed to be successful and prevent old habits from resurfacing [25].

When dealing with bariatric surgery as a resource to lose weight, previous research has found positive associations between postoperatory support and weight loss. It seems that to make significant lifestyle adjustments, education and face-to-face support are needed to cope with stress and prevent relapses [26]. But what happens with those patients that have no time to attend the meetings or are too shy to join a support group? Can digital technology provide a solution for them?

With the advent of instant mobile messaging applications such as Telegram and Whatsapp, people have adopted a new way to communicate with each other and to manage their health. Nowadays, individuals are comfortable addressing a health concern with a doctor or sharing a photo related to a personal health problem using their mobile phones. These facts have been considered as an advantage by physicians, health coaches, and psychologists who use the mobile phones and the apps to deliver specific interventions, advice, and counseling to enhance their patients' health. At the same time, apps such as Whatsapp and Telegram provide patients with free tools to have private conversations to share their most personal concerns and build a community of think-alike supporters.

5.2.1. The method

To shed more light on the use of instant mobile messaging applications in-depth interviews were conducted with five adult women who decided to go into bariatric surgery to lose weight and improve their health. A semistructured questionnaire was used to identify their behaviors and motivations related with health issues and social support. They were also asked about the benefits they receive from using Telegram and/or Whatsapp to be in touch with their doctors and peers. In-depth interviews were recorded, transcribed, and analyzed [27], and the findings are presented in the following section.

5.2.2. The findings

The in-depth interviews allowed us an understanding of the facts that motivate bariatric surgery patients to use instant messaging applications. The five subjects of our study are patients of a bariatric surgeon in the North of Mexico. In fact, it was the doctor who suggested the patients to join a Whatsapp group in order to provide them—along with 340 more patients—consistent and standardized psychological and nutritional advice, designed specifically for bariatric patients.

Our findings suggest that this Whatsapp group offers several advantages, as well as some limitations. The first, and most important, reason to use the group is the presence of three health specialists that conform the bariatric team: the surgeon, a psychologist, and a nutritionist. Having a bariatric team present allows participants to receive supervised support from licensed health providers, who are familiar with each patient case and have the knowledge and experience to provide instrumental and informational support.

Since most persons obtained information for bariatric surgery from friends, there is a need to educate them in several topics, such as grocery shopping, meal preparation, and how to deal with meal times, among other issues. In this group, participants find specific advice on the process of acquiring—and maintaining—a new lifestyle. The nutritionist shares food recipes and provides tips on how to get all the nutritional requirements with less food and even suggests which restaurants to visit and what meals to order when dining out.

The common person believes that bariatric surgery is a magical solution for obesity. But the surgery is only the first step in achieving a long-term change. A bariatric surgery patient has to deal with several considerations, therefore, the need to have professional support before and after the procedure. Before the surgery, most patients have mixed feelings: they want the surgery to improve their quality of life and look better, but at the same time, they are scared and fear operative and postoperative complications.

Our findings suggest that being a member of the Whatsapp group before the surgery allows patients to reduce preoperatory stress and feel confident that the surgery will be a successful event. It seems that being in touch with individuals who already went into the surgery provides new patients with a sense of security and provides enough motivation to continue with the procedure.

After the surgery, other concerns arise. In the first days, some individuals feel ill, have nausea, and are afraid to eat to avoid having an upset stomach. Besides, bariatric surgery patients have to stick to a new diet, which includes limitations on what or how much to eat. In the first weeks, the technical advice and support of the nutritionist is very important. Our sample reported being anxious for not having enough knowledge about food and its nutritional value. While most of them were concerned about food calories before the surgery to avoid gaining weight, now their main concern is if they are having enough nutrients to nourish their bodies and have a healthy lifestyle.

The presence of other patients in the group is valuable in this stage. More experienced patients have already acquired the knowledge and experience to deal with food issues. They have tested several recipes, have a selection of restaurants that serve half portions or small portions, and are willing to share their findings with new patients.

The five interviewed women use the Whatsapp group more than three times a week. They find the support useful and want to be in touch with the bariatric team in a constant way. But they find some limitations: the group is very large (more than 340 patients, plus the health care team); therefore, some conversation threads get lost, there is confusion with some answers, and some members of the group make irrelevant comments or include jokes, photos, or messages that do not support the main goal of the group.

The surgeon also created a Facebook group to provide patients with new forms of support. Videos, food recipes, and photos are published on a daily base, allowing members of the community to easily find specific and useful content for their needs. Additionally in this Facebook group, the surgeon publishes photos of patients who have reached a milestone (i.e., a weight goal). These posts serve as motivators for new patients and provide an environment to receive applause and recognition when a milestone is accomplished. We found that positive comments and words of encouragement are important for bariatric surgery patients, especially for those who suffered from low self-esteem before the surgery or were victims of criticism and isolation for being overweight.

Even though the patients we interviewed affirm that the main reason for going into bariatric surgery was to improve their health, they acknowledge the psychological benefits of losing weight as well. They now feel more confident and attractive; feel free to use more fashionable clothes and lead an active social life.

Given the limitations of the large Whatsapp group, 15 female bariatric surgery patients living in the same city in the North of Mexico created a new and smaller group using Telegram, which allows them to encrypt their comments and have a more personal conversation with women who live in the same area and have access to similar gyms, restaurants, and other service facilities.

The five subjects of our study are active participants in this Telegram group. They join the conversation on a daily base to share advice, exchange recipes, encourage each other, and even setting dates to meet at the gym and exercise together. Participants in the study affirm that Telegram is easy to use, is very appealing because it allows private messages within the group, and is reliable and affordable.

In sum, the five bariatric surgery patients believe Telegram and Whatsapp offer them a window of opportunities to be in touch with a team of experts, that provide constant counseling that includes education, coping strategies, and adjustment advice to achieve and maintain a new lifestyle. In these groups, they feel cared and understood by their virtual friends—who in many cases, become real friends—the comments they receive are always positive and encouraging and allow them to face the anxiety and even the depression of being overweight.

5.3. There is an app for that

The market has a wide offer of technological devices that mounted on the wrist, ankle, or belt of the user track their physical activities, including sleep hours, steps taken, and stairs climbed. Other devices accurately monitor pulse, blood glucose, and stress levels. These wearable devices allow individuals to monitor their health and fitness on a daily basis and have the benefit of creating a dashboard that allows comparison, goal tracking, and even sharing the information with friends and health experts. Some of these devices can be used with specific apps to help users achieve specific health-related goals. There are apps designed for those who want to quit smoking, exercise more, eat healthy or monitor their sleep patterns and stressful moments, and many of them are were built following BE principles, allowing the provision of feedback, triggers, nudges, and rewards [15].

5.3.1. The method

To explore how individuals use wearable devices, smartphones, and apps we conducted five in-depth interviews with graduate students who are interested in doing physical activity and eating a healthy diet to achieve overall physical wellbeing. A semistructured questionnaire was designed to identify their behaviors, and we also asked them to share with us the information provided by the apps' dashboards and explain us the advantages of using those specific apps and wearable devices.

http://dx.doi.org/10.5772/67768

5.3.2. *The findings*

Participants in the study use branded apps (e.g., Nike running) and apps designed by private developers that are offered in the Android and Apple stores. It seems that the subjects of our study prefer apps built with specific scientific knowledge basis like the Transtheoretical Model of Change, which states that behavior change unfold through six different stages: pre-contemplation, contemplation, preparation, action, maintenance, and termination [28]. These types of apps were designed to acknowledge the typical problems an individual faces when trying to quit smoking or engaging into a healthy diet; therefore, as seen by users as a complete set of tools that will help them achieve and maintain the desired behavior.

The most preferred apps offer tools to create social groups, initiate challenges, provide virtual badges when the user reaches a milestone, and offer real-world rewards (such as cash and points to exchange for merchandise at selected stores) to increase engagement and provide external motivation. The apps offer clear dashboards that allow the users to visualize their goals, their achievements, and compare their results with other individuals, creating a friendly competition among users.

Our participants perceive that wearable devices and health-monitoring apps increase their self-efficacy to attain their goals. They appreciate the accurate feedback and the reminders and nudges that help them keep on track. Wearable devices have become an important item of their wardrobe and help them present a distinctive image in their social groups, letting them show their interests and hobbies with specific products such as a watch, a pair of sneakers, or a bracelet.

At the same time, most of the apps can be synchronized with SNS to share the dashboards' data with virtual friends. Sharing exercise information and earned badges affects feelings of connectedness among members of the SNS. This specific feature allows users to receive feedback from their peers, encouragement when they are running a race, and applause when they reach a milestone. For others, the posts serve as a reminder of their own goals and act as a form of pressure to keep going. App users believe the benefit of sharing information on SNS is mutual: they feel not only challenged by peers to achieve their goals but also perceive themselves as influencers setting a good example for their virtual friends to embrace healthier behaviors. We found that the interaction between apps, SNS, and members of a community provides psychological gratification in the form of network support and social incentives.

6. Not everything is sunny and bright: limitations and shortcomings

The content analysis also revealed some limitations and shortcomings of SNS, virtual groups, and health-monitoring apps, which are listed as follows:

(a) Safety and privacy—Participants in the study show their concern regarding their privacy and safety. Most of them are sharing photos and personal information, which could be misused by hackers or exposes them to threats and cybercrime.

(b) Unwanted sell calls—Opportunistic people are everywhere, and SNS are not the exception. In the studied communities, we found several posts trying to sell different health-related articles, which were seen as unwanted intrusion by participants.

(c) Irrelevant comments and posts—Not all participants have the same goal when joining a virtual community and that fact is reflected in their posts (e.g., jokes, nonrelated pictures).

(d) Reliability and trust—Individuals who chose to join a social support community are seeking for reliable advice. As one participant said during the interviews: "If I see that a virtual friend liked a post in Facebook I take it as a personal recommendation. If he/she likes a product I think that he/she has tried the article and his/her like becomes a reliable source of advice for me."

(e) Accuracy of data—Traditional apps require users to self-fed information regarding their habits and behaviors; some individuals might make involuntary mistakes while recording information; therefore, the provided feedback will not be accurate.

(f) Use it or it won't work—People have to log in to the SNS to seek and receive the support, individuals have to wear their smart watches or smart bands in order to monitor their behaviors and receive the feedback.

The presence of a community manager can help overcome some of the limitations presented above. Unwanted members of the community can be eliminated and irrelevant posts can be erased. Also, a clear policy on what can be posted will help resolve some of the shortcomings.

Regarding the accuracy of data, it is important to educate users of wearable devices and apps and show them how to register information and how to measure different things (e.g., the amount of food).

Prizes and rewards can be employed to motivate people to use their apps or visit the virtual communities. But finally, we have to acknowledge that the use of SNS, wearable devices, and apps is a personal choice, and people will exert their right to engage with them or not.

7. Conclusion

The high costs of health care, the lack of time to visit the doctor on a regular basis, and the growing interest to prevent illness and diseases are some of the factors that motivate individuals to take health care into their own hands and that can be achieved with the use of technology. The use of apps to monitor exercise and calorie intake seems to be popular among participants in the studied Facebook communities, as well as in the group of runners. Nowadays, apps can be linked to SNS; therefore, individuals receive immediate feedback both from the apps and from their peers in their SNS. Sharing exercise information and badges affects feelings of connectedness among members of the communities, provides a tool that can be used to encourage others to change their current behavior and engage in a healthier one, and motivates individuals to aim higher in terms of exercise goals. By using specific tools like Telegram to create small communities, individuals find a network conformed of peers that have similar problems and that provide an empathic advice that sometimes is hard to find with relatives and friends. Health apps, therefore, can be used to design specific health marketing interventions. In summary, digital technologies can assist individuals in making good decisions that lead to healthy outcomes.

Appendices and nomenclatures

App	Smartphone application
BE	Behavioral economics
mHealth	Mobile health
SNS	Social network sites

Author details

Alicia De la Pena* and Bernardo Amezcua

*Address all correspondence to: mktgheraldo@yahoo.com.mx

Universidad Autónoma de Coahuila, Saltillo, México

References

[1] Ajzen I. The theory of planned behavior. Organizational Behavior and Human Decision Processes. 1991;50(2):179-211.

[2] Thaler R., Sunstein C. Nudge. 1st ed. New Haven, Connecticut: Yale University Press; 2008.

[3] Heaney C., Israel B. Social networks and social support. In: Glanz K., Kimer B., Viswanath K., ed. by. Health Behavior and Health Education. 1st ed. California: Jossey-Bass; 2008. pp. 189-210.

[4] Kozinets R. Netnography. 1st ed. Los Angeles, California: SAGE; 2010.

[5] Spiggle S. Analysis and interpretation of qualitative data in consumer research. Journal of Consumer Research. 1994;21(3):491.

[6] The State of Mobile Apps [Internet]. Nielsen.com. 2010 [cited 19 January 2017]. Available from: http://www.nielsen.com/us/en/reports/2010/The-State-Of-Mobile-Apps.html.

[7] Nielsen. Reports and Insights | Mobile Consumer Report [Internet]. Nielsen.com. 2013 [cited 19 January 2017]. Available from: http://www.nielsen.com/us/en/reports/2013/mobile-consumer-report-february-2013.html.

[8] IPSOS. Our Mobile Planet: Understanding the Mobile Consumer | Ipsos [Internet]. Ipsos.com.cn. 2012 [cited 30 May 2016]. Available from: http://www.ipsos.com.cn/en/node/2760.

[9] Todd P., Rogers Y., Payne S. Nudging the trolley in the supermarket: how to deliver the right information to shoppers. In: Lumsden J., ed. by. Developments in Technologies for Human-Centric Mobile Computing and Applications [Internet]. 1st ed. Hersheys, PA: IGI Global; 2012 [cited 4 January 2017]. pp. 99-113.

[10] Coughlin, S., Wordham, J. Rising Consumerism: Winning the Hearts and Minds of Health Care Consumers [Internet]. Dupress.deloitte.com. 2015 [cited 10 December 2016]. Available from: https://dupress.deloitte.com/dup-us-en/deloitte-review/issue-16/consumerism-health-care.html.

[11] Davenport, T., Lucker, J. Running on Data: Activity Trackers and the Internet of Things [Internet]. Dupress.deloitte.com. 2015 [cited 9 November 2016]. Available from: https://dupress.deloitte.com/dup-us-en/deloitte-review/issue-16/internet-of-things-wearable-technology.html.

[12] Drell L. An App a Day Keeps the Doctor Away [Internet]. Ama.org. 2014 [cited 10 November 2016]. Available from: https://www.ama.org/publications/MarketingHealthServices/Pages/app-a-day-keeps-doctor-away.aspx.

[13] mHealth New Horizons for Health Through Mobile Technologies [Internet]. Who.int. 2011 [cited 10 November 2016]. Available from: http://www.who.int/goe/publications/goe_mhealth_web.pdf.

[14] Fox S., Duggan M. Health Online 2013 [Internet]. Pewinternet.org. 2013 [cited 10 November 2016]. Available from: http://www.pewinternet.org/2013/01/15/health-online-2013/.

[15] Patel M., Asch D., Volpp K. Wearable devices as facilitators, not drivers, of health behavior change. JAMA. 2015;313(5):459.

[16] Ba S., Wang L. Digital health communities: the effect of their motivation mechanisms. Decision Support Systems. 2013;55(4):941-947.

[17] Katz A. Self-help and mutual aid: an emerging social movement? Annual Review of Sociology. 1981;7(1):129-155.

[18] Moisio R., Beruchashvili M. Questing for well-being at weight watchers: the role of the spiritual-therapeutic model in a support group. Journal of Consumer Research. 2010;36(5):857-875.

[19] Belk R. Extended self in a digital world. Journal of Consumer Research. 2013;40(3):477-500.

[20] Burke M., Settles B. Plugged in to the community: social motivators in online goal-setting groups. Proceedings of the 5th International Conference on Communities and Technologies [Internet]. Dl.acm.org; 2011 [cited 12 January 2017]. Available from: http://burrsettles.com/pub/burke.ct11.pdf.

[21] Scaraboto D., Rossi C., Costa D. How consumers persuade each other: rhetorical strategies of interpersonal influence in online communities. BAR, Brazilian Administration Review. 2012;9(3):246-267.

[22] Ariely D. The end of rational economics [Internet]. Harvard Business Review. 2009 [cited 2 January 2017]. Available from: https://hbr.org/2009/07/the-end-of-rational-economics.

[23] Keller P., Lehmann D. Designing effective health communications: a meta-analysis. Journal of Public Policy & Marketing. 2008;27(2):117-130.

[24] Top 20 Facebook Statistics—Updated January 2017 [Internet]. Zephoria.com. 2017 [cited 12 January 2017]. Available from: https://zephoria.com/top-15-valuable-facebook-statistics/.

[25] Buchwald, H. and Williams, S. Bariatric surgery worldwide 2003. Obesity Surgery. 2004;14(9):1157-1164.

[26] Livhits, M., Mercado, C., Yermilov, I., Parikh, J., Dutson, E., Mehran, A., Ko, C., Shekelle, P. and Gibbons, M. Is social support associated with greater weight loss after bariatric surgery? A systematic review. Obesity Reviews. 2011;12(2):142-148.

[27] Guest, G. How many interviews are enough? An experiment with data saturation and variability. Field Methods. 2006; 18(1): 59-82.

[28] Prochaska J., Velicer W. The transtheoretical model of health behavior change. American Journal of Health Promotion. 1997;12(1):38-48.

Chapter 8

Universal Health Coverage and Environmental Health: An Investigation in Decreasing Communicable and Chronic Disease by Including Environmental Health in UHC

Muhiuddin Haider and Katrina Bibb

Additional information is available at the end of the chapter

http://dx.doi.org/10.5772/intechopen.69922

Abstract

Over 83% of major diseases are environmentally mediated. These environmental factors include access to clean air and water, nutritional food, adequate shelter and access to health care. As health care systems across the globe struggle to include not only preventive health, but also health literacy in their approaches, it has become apparent that the most feasible system to combine all of these necessities is the universal health care/coverage (UHC) approach. This system also ensures that everyone has access to health services without financial hardship. It is imperative that environmental health (EH) is included in this approach, however, considering the global burden of disease due to environmental health factors. Epidemiological evidence-based approaches such as Water, Sanitation and Hygiene (WASH), have proven the advantage of utilizing these environmental health practices. In order to integrate EH into UHC, a dual multipronged (preventive and clinical) approach can be implemented; however, many are using a multisectoral approach due to the array of public-private partnerships which aid in its success. In alignment with the Millennium and Sustainable Development Goals, nations must make strides to address health disparities, chronic disease and poverty. Low and middle income countries (LMIC) are disproportionately burdened by economic insecurity, global pollution and preexisting issues within their government infrastructure, creating the worst health outcomes in these nations. Bangladesh has some of the worst chronic disease morbidities in the world due to indoor air pollution, rural and urban health disparities and food insecurity. Although the nation has begun to integrate EH into UHC, better coordination among ministries implementing health care is necessary, along with increased monetary allocation from the government. There is also a dire need for more health care providers who possess appropriate skills to work in the public sector. Lastly, more equitable access to services in both rural and urban areas and an improved financing mechanism must be instilled to successfully implement this EH/UHC approach.

Keywords: universal health care, universal health coverage, UHC, multipronged approach, multisectoral approach, environmental health, noncommunicable disease, NCD, chronic disease, communicable disease, morbidity, mortality, global disease burden, Millennium Development Goals (MDGs), Sustainable Development Goals (SDGs), Bangladesh

1. Introduction

According to the World Health Organization (WHO), it is estimated that over 100 million people are forced into poverty every year due to out-of-pocket health care expenditures [1]. Although there are numerous factors, including but not limited to social status, environmental agents and cultural aspects, which may contribute to an individual's susceptibility to this statistic, implementing universal health coverage (UHC)[1] would undoubtedly help to diminish this number. By working toward this type of system to ensure good health, economic growth will also follow, benefitting communities holistically rather than unilaterally [2].

The objective of universal health coverage is to ensure that "all people can use health services without financial hardship" [1]. In order for this to be attained successfully, governmental health financing systems must be put into place and encourage collaboration among different governmental levels and agencies. Implementing a UHC system would lessen the gap between rich and poor communities by ensuring health equity, unlike the free market system. The ultimate purpose of UHC, therefore, would be to lower both the disease and financial burden at the community level by providing adequate preventive and clinical health care services to all.

In terms of prevention, environmental health (EH) factors should be addressed within the service-oriented nature of UHC, due to their high attribution to disease [3]. Through counseling and behavioral change models, environmental health factors such as exposures to contaminated air and water can be prevented. Educating communities on these environmental exposures through UHC infrastructure is paramount in successfully addressing these issues and bettering community health. Furthermore, environmental epidemiology is a useful tool in providing evidence-based science to illustrate these successes; Water, Sanitation and Hygiene (WASH) programs via clinics have provided health education counseling on this practice, therefore exponentially decreased infectious and enteric diseases [4].

2. Universal health coverage

The fundamental principle of UHC can be found in the 1948 United Nations Universal Declaration of Human Rights constitution; it states that, "Everyone has a right to a standard of living adequate for the health and well-being of himself and of his family, including food,

[1]Universal Health Coverage can be used synonymously with Universal Health Care—in this manuscript, UHC can in turn be used to reference either phrase.

clothing, household and medical care and necessary social services" [5]. Following this precedent, the Alma-Ata Declaration developed its "Health for All" agenda in 1978, declaring equity to be of utmost importance [5]. In order to make this system feasible, a number of components must be present.

Firstly, the system must be robust and well developed in order to run efficiently and meet all of the priority health needs of its community members. It also must be focused on people-centered, integrated care with foci in both preventive medicine and clinical evaluation and treatment. Primary services should be focused on both communicable and noncommunicable diseases (NCDs), along with maternal and child health. This can be accomplished by: engaging community members through trusting relationships, screening/early detection methods, ensuring capacity to treat diagnosed diseases and providing therapeutic and/or rehabilitative services. The system must also be affordable so that financial hardships are alleviated and equity is achieved; different funding mechanisms to accomplish this are abundant and can be personalized per country. Consequently, a system cannot clearly be implemented without the accessibility to treatments; therefore, there must be access to crucial medicines and other technologies necessary to diagnose and/or treat conditions. Lastly, a sufficient team of trained and passionate healthcare workers, including but not limited to physicians, nurses, community health care workers and health educators (this team may vary depending on patients' needs), grounded in the best available evidence [5].

The UHC system also requires strategic interventions to address the most paramount causes of disease and mortality. As aforementioned, a wide array of quality health services should be covered involving health promotion, preventive care, clinical treatment, rehabilitation services and palliative care. In order to decide which area takes priority, epidemiological data and context are leveraged along with health systems, socioeconomic development and individuals' expectations [6].

Data have shown that over 83% of major diseases reported by WHO are environmentally mediated [3]. Considering this high attribution, environmental health has become a topic of utmost concern in addressing disease morbidity and mortality. In terms of UHC, preventive care and health promotion have become important foci to address these environmental health disease etiologies (see Appendix A for additional explanatory **Figures 6** and **7**). To better understand the role of environmental health and how to successfully address this disease burden, socioeconomic and racial factors contributing to health disparities much be investigated. Health literacy and access to clean air and water via an individual's built (surrounding) environment are major sources of exposure that have led to high morbidities in developing countries. The main objective in investigating environmental health is to decide which aspects to focus on in UHC, how to successfully communicate these practices and change detrimental behaviors and, lastly, to make the solutions sustainable.

The objective of this paper is to provide the analytical framework for health care systems to integrate environmental health into universal health care. As aforementioned, environmental health accounts for the vast majority of major disease etiologies, therefore, justifying the rationale for making it an imperative part of UHC. The current problem exists in the fact that UHC does not address environmental health; this will later be illustrated within the case study on UHC in Bangladesh. This paper will also provide the framework on how to incorporate environmental health into UHC using both the two-pronged approach and the multipronged/multisectoral approach as feasible solutions.

3. Environmental health

EH is the science behind preventing injury and detrimental exposure to environmental agents that may be physical, chemical, biological or social/cultural. These agents are transmitted primarily by air, water, soil or food [7]. Social/cultural burdens include socioeconomic status (SES), race, ethnicity or any other practices that limit one's social environment or access to healthcare. These factors can be exacerbated by health inequity and the state of climate change, that is, access to healthy and untainted food and water considering one's built environment. EH also includes the assessment and control of disease with environmental etiologies as well, especially those such as vector-borne illnesses such as malaria or diarrheal diseases. The objective is to prevent disease and create health-promoting environments (see Appendix A for additional explanatory **Figures 6** and **7**).

From an epidemiological perspective, because environmental heath factors can occur at the individual, household, community, regional and global levels, EH issues have a great impact on global disease burden [6]. As a whole, it is estimated that environmental risk factors contribute to between 25% and 33% of the global disease burden (**Figure 1**) [8, 9]. Moreover, these environmental risk factors can be broken down into communicable versus noncommunicable linkages.

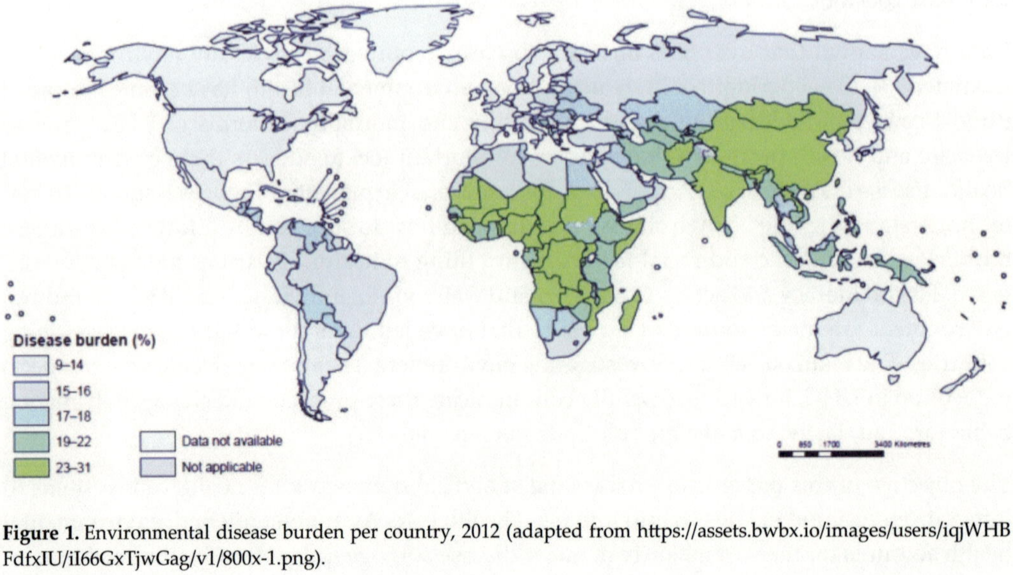

Figure 1. Environmental disease burden per country, 2012 (adapted from https://assets.bwbx.io/images/users/iqjWHBFdfxIU/iI66GxTjwGag/v1/800x-1.png).

Noncommunicable diseases kill 38 million people per year. Furthermore, nearly three-quarters of these diseases occur in low and middle income countries (LMIC), providing evidence for inequity. Some of the major noncommunicable diseases identified by WHO due to their mortality include cardiovascular disease, cancer, respiratory disease and diabetes [10]. Air pollution, particularly particulate matter (PM) from traffic, cooking stoves and incineration, to name a few environmental etiologies, has been linked to cardiovascular disease in a number of epidemiological studies over the past decade [11]. Cancer can be linked to a plethora of toxic chemicals found anywhere from personal care products and cleaning products and to crops contaminated with toxic molds; many of these can be found on the United States Agency for Toxic Substances and Disease Registry (ATSDR) Priority List, signifying their significance in terms of human exposure, toxicity and frequency of exposure [12]. Respiratory diseases can also be linked to chemical exposure and similar etiologies of cardiovascular disease, that is, air pollution (tobacco smoke and PM), exposure to asbestos and other occupational trade industry exposures (wood and leather dust) [13]. Conclusively, diabetes can clearly be linked to individuals' access to healthy food (food deserts) and their ability to maintain a well-balanced diet. Food deserts are a global health equity issue, also found in even high-income countries such as the USA.

Alternatively, communicable diseases, otherwise known as infectious diseases, are found almost entirely in LMIC. Major risk factors for these outbreaks include flooding, likely caused by global warming and climate change. Flooding contaminates drinking water sources and stimulates mold growth in both crop fields and containers holding water or crops, which leads to an array of water-borne diseases and epidemics including cholera, hepatitis A, typhoid fever and leptospirosis. Additionally, due to the attraction of insects, namely mosquitos, to these environments, vector-borne diseases such as Ebola, dengue, malaria, yellow fever, gangue hemorrhagic fever and West Nile fever have all increased exponentially. Developmental birth defects such as neural tube defects (NTDs) can also result from these diseases, that is, the Zika virus and microcephaly. The lack of availability to clean water also leads to diarrheal disease and ear, nose and throat infections. Additionally, social/cultural practices can contribute to transmission of disease such as the practice of burning an Ebola corpse, which occurred in the Ebola epidemic most recently. Tuberculosis can also be transmitted by corpses along with other blood-borne viruses and gastrointestinal infections [14]. Some communicable diseases can also be contracted at rapid rates by the built environment, for example, tuberculosis, influenza and other air-borne disease causing agents due to overcrowding—prisons in countries such as Russia and slums in many other countries, namely India.

To put the health equity across countries in perspective, in LMIC, lower respiratory infections are the third leading cause of death, while chronic obstructive pulmonary disease (COPD) is the sixth leading cause of death. Disproportionately, when looking at children between the ages of 0 and 14, lower respiratory disease is actually ranked second, while diarrheal disease is ranked third [6]. Globally, more than a third of the disease burden due to environmental factors falls on children [15]. Considering all of these environmental risk factors, the top risk factors have been identified as unimproved water and sanitation and air pollution.

4. Global initiatives

Due to the continuous interaction between the environment and poor health outcomes, the following global development goals have been identified as contributors/targets to address environmental health. Clearly, environmental stability must be the ultimate goal to alleviate the aforementioned environmentally mediated diseases; in order to accomplish this, however, both poverty and poor baseline health must be addressed [16]. Each goal includes a number of target objectives and timeframes to accomplish in order to alleviate detrimental aspects of each goal.

4.1. Millennium Development Goals

All of the eight main Millennium Development Goals (MDGs) are applicable to driving EH practices in countries that are part of the UN. Additionally, considering the weight they carry globally, this further justifies the need to include EH within UHC. The main Goal (7) is to ensure environmental sustainability. To ensure sustainability within one's environment is to provide a healthy built environment, free of excess disease and risk factors. Secondly, Goal (4) is to reduce child mortality. This goal is one of utmost importance due to the fat that over a third of the global disease burden falls on children [15]. Goal (1), which aims to eradicate extreme poverty and hunger, is also directly related to environmental health. Similarly to children's high risk, disproportionate burdens of disease cultivate among groups with low SES exacerbating the disease burden; this is a primary focus considering communicable diseases and their high rates of transmission, especially in areas of low SES. Furthermore, Goals (3) and (5) align with gender equality and empowering women/improving maternal health. This vulnerable group, alongside children and low income, also is especially susceptible to disproportionate levels of environmental risk factors, that is, indoor smoke from cooking and childbirth complications. The need for EH within UHC to lessen this disparity and risk is vital, especially in developing countries where access to care and cultural norms prove to be additional obstacles to ensure good health. Of course, Goal (6), to combat HIV/AIDS, malaria and other diseases, has a direct correlation to EH prevention strategies. Additionally, more educated mothers have been shown to have fewer and healthier children [17]. This is directly correlating MDG Goal (2), which is aimed at achieving universal primary education. Lastly, global partnerships for development, Goal (8), are an important concept, especially within lower income countries. As shown previously, disease burden is disproportionately high in these countries, causing stress on both the communities and the economies. The need for better infrastructure and aid from higher income countries is an important factor to consider, despite the fact that this goal is not directly correlated to in country UHC and EH. In country, multisectoral approaches can help lessen this stress partially also.

4.2. Sustainable Development Goals

The Sustainable Development Goals (SDGs) were created in 2015 by the United Nations and are significant in addressing environmental exposures and therefore decreasing morbidity and mortality. By creating clean, sustainable environments and teaching individuals healthy practices, environmentally mediated diseases associated with the previously mentioned diseases and poor health outcomes, that is, cholera, diarrhea, COPD, cancer, adverse birth outcomes, etc., can be addressed in a global, systematic manner. The burden of many of these diseases, both communicable and noncommunicable, can be alleviated in part by the MDG and SDG. These goals are the driving force for sustainable environmental health practices in countries that are part of the UN.

All of the SDGs can also be utilized to show the need for EH integration within UHC, as they have a direct correlation to EH and sustainability. They include: Goal (3) good health and well-being, Goal (6) clean water sanitation, Goal (13) combat climate change and impact, Goal (7) affordable and clean energy, Goal (9) industry, innovation and infrastructure, Goal (11) sustainable communities, Goal (12) responsible consumerism and production and lastly, Goals (14) and (15) life below water and on land. Specific examples of their exposures can be found previously in the EH section, that is, climate change and flooding, toxicological exposures within food, and morbidity and mortality of pollution sources.

Figure 2 shows the contrasting distribution of all major communicable and noncommunicable diseases (and injuries) across countries. The figure illustrates the disproportionate burden these majorly environmental mediated communicable diseases have on LMIC, namely Africa. Most importantly, however, it shows the prevalence of noncommunicable (chronic) disease across these countries in relationship to the disability adjusted life years (DALYs), which illustrate overall disease burden. Although communicable diseases disproportionately burden LMIC, overburdening of NCDs is found among all countries, despite economic status.

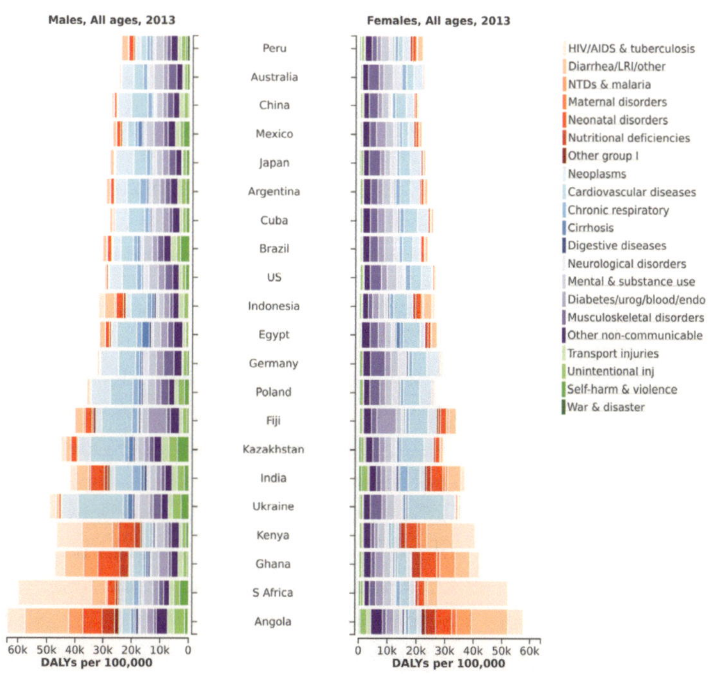

Figure 2. Burden of disease by cause, country, and gender (2013 estimates)—produced by IHME Viz Hub (adapted from https://ourworldindata.org/burden-of-disease/).

5. Intersection

5.1. Environmental health through UHC

Considering the high burden of environmental factors on human disease, universal health coverage can be accomplished significantly through improving environmental health. This is especially true in the aspects of health promotion and disease prevention within UHC. Conclusively, as mentioned previously within the EH section, the main aspects of environmental health that can be investigated in this aspect include:

- Indoor and outdoor pollution—that is, air pollution leading to respiratory issues
- Food safety—that is, mold growth due to climate change (flooding) and cancer
- Hygiene and sanitation—that is, need for clean water to lessen diarrheal diseases
- Vector control—that is, to mitigate vector-borne diseases such as dengue and Zika virus
- Solid waste management—that is, to ensure that water sources are not contaminated
- Occupational health and industrial hygiene—that is, understanding higher occupational exposures and ensuring worker safety across governmental agencies

These major environmentally mediated global health issues can be integrated into UHC, utilizing the "two Pronged" approach, which includes both (1) preventive and (2) treatment aspects [6]. The preventive portion invests in education and major infrastructure, that is, sewage, water treatment and scrubbers on coal-fired boilers. The services included in the prevention aspect also include health education and delivery of services to communities who are challenged in their access to appropriate health care. On the other hand, the treatment side integrates both environmental and occupational health data into the physician's assessment alongside ability and resources in order to "prescribe" reduced exposures, that is, mold within the household and occupational allergens [6]. This could also be viewed as a pre- versus post-exposure scenario, with the main focus on mitigating environmental health exposures.

This two-pronged approach can better address environmental health by focusing on the service aspect. As aforementioned, access to health care is a major issue in both developing countries and even developed countries, which encompasses health disparities, primarily due to SES. In order to address these components, the appropriate services must be offered. In some cases, diagnostic tests may prove useful in prescribing correct medications for communicable diseases, while consultations in prevention measures for environmental exposures can be effective in others. It is without a doubt that health consultations from community health care workers and ideally primary health care (PHC) providers should be a priority. PHC is important to assess the patient's health in a holistic manner and applies the most appropriate service. Diagnostics tests may be out of reach for individuals in resource-limited countries and/or low-income areas, however, proving the need for a different service delivery system. Global initiatives (MDG and SDG) can aid in lessening the disease burden overall, therefore applying less pressure to localized services. It is plausible to utilize epidemiological methods to inform global or even national policy in order to reduce exposures. This would lessen the economic and resource burdens at the local level.

5.2. Integrating environmental health with UHC

Because of the fact that health insurance alone cannot mitigate all of these environmental health factors, a "multipronged" approach has been suggested to alleviate this issue. In general, the three pillars of this approach include (1) responding to existing demand, (2) anticipating healthcare needs and (3) addressing underlying (structural) issues. Responding to demand is imperative in order to provide affordable, equitable high-quality health services from a pluralistic health system. Secondly, in an era of rapid growth and both health and social transition, anticipating community health care needs is an imperative factor to account for. Lastly, in order to make a sustainable system, underlying issues must be addressed to ensure progress [6]. The variance of these three pillars can be personalized per country for optimal success [18, 19]. A recent report by the World Bank Report on universal health coverage for Inclusive and Sustainable Development shows the diversity of this approach. As seen in **Figure 3**, countries in Groups 2 and 3 have implemented or are working toward a multipronged approach [19]. **Figure 3** illustrates the diversity of this approach and flexibility in order to meet the needs of a particular nation. Bangladesh is seen in Group 1 as a pilot multipronged approach to UHC. This case study will be discussed in the next section; it is important to follow early stage programs and survey their effectiveness in UHC.

A "multisectoral" approach could also be employed to include environmental heath factors. This can be accomplished by engaging other instrumentalities of universal health care including (1) health care delivery systems, (2) individuals within the health workforce, (3) health facilities and/or communication networks and (4) governmental agencies and legislators. Delivery systems, health workforce and communication networks can be primarily effective in spreading awareness and mobilizing efforts at the community level, within households. This

	Group 1	*Group 2*	*Group 3*	*Group 4*
Status of UHC policies and programs	Agenda setting; piloting new programs and developing new systems	Initial programs and systems in place, implementation in progress; need for further systems development and capacity building to address remaining uncovered population	Strong political leadership and citizen demand lead to new investments and UHC policy reforms; systems and programs develop to meet new demands	Mature systems and programs: adaptive systems enable continuous adjustments to meet changing demands
Status of health coverage	Low population coverage; at the early stage of UHC	Significant share of population gain access to services with financial protection, but population coverage is not yet universal and coverage gaps in access to services and financial protection remain	Universal population coverage achieved but countries are focusing on improving financial protection and quality of services	Universal coverage sustained with comprehensive access to health services and effective financial protection
Participating countries	Bangladesh Ethiopia	Ghana Indonesia Peru Vietnam	Brazil Thailand Turkey	France Japan

Note: UHC = universal health coverage.

Figure 3. UHC program countries (adapted from http://apps.who.int/medicinedocs/documents/s21582en/s21582en.pdf).

could educate individuals on the importance of environmental health, including sanitation and ventilation, especially when using indoor cook stoves fueled by biomass [20]. Alternatives such as kerosene or gas energy sources could be encouraged along with handwashing techniques and the use of mosquito nets to lessen vector-borne disease. The use of outreach infrastructure could also be vital in integrating networks from microcredit activities with environmental health initiatives [6].

Utilizing pertinent governmental agencies and legislators is also invaluable to integrating environmental health in specific trades and in general occupational health practices. This relationship to individuals with power could also make equipment available, or aid in subsidizing the purchase of, which aims to improve environmental health, that is, gas-powered stoves, mosquito nets and water sanitation systems. Legislation could be developed and implemented in specific areas for the safety of large groups, for instance, food safety, waste management and occupational health. Policy could too be integrated with local government to support public-private partnerships; Ministries of Public Health, Ministry of Health, Ministry of Environment or Forest/Agriculture and Ministry of Education can all be leveraged here. With support from these powers, community-level efforts to spread awareness about the importance of environmental health in order to control the burden and spread of disease could be a long-term solution to alleviate these health-deteriorating factors. Unfortunately, education will not be the end all solution, however, due to the interconnectivity of universal poverty. Ensuring access to healthy environments is vital in one's overall health to mitigate environmental health factors, which leads to NCDs and a wide array of chronic diseases that put many people out of work and into poverty.

6. Case study: Bangladesh

In a country whose population exceeds 156 million people and is embedded deep within South Asia (a continent that contains of nearly 40% of the world's poverty) it is a feat that they have accomplished so much over the past four decades [21, 22]. With the help of the World Health Organization, Bangladesh has met a multitude of Millennium Development Goals over these four decades, particularly in terms of maternal and child health. Maternal mortality and both infant and child mortality along with malnutrition have all declined [23]. Concurrently, poverty rates and the number of people living in hunger have declined up to 30% since the 1970s as well [22]. All of these factors have also helped individuals to live longer; the life expectancy in Bangladesh (70 years) exceeds the global average of 69 years [23]. Despite these facts and the future promise they bring, there are still major public health problems that persist in Bangladesh, especially in terms of environmental health.

Bangladesh still ranks in the bottom four countries for maternal health [23]. This may be due to a number of delays in giving birth including the social/cultural decision to come to the health care facility, issue of transportation in getting to the facility and the question of whether the health care facility has the adequate services to aid in delivery (midwives, medications, ability to perform blood transfusions, etc.) Additionally, although child malnutrition is decreasing, poor nutrition is still a main issue of concern, considering that nearly half of Bangladeshi children prior to 1-year-old and up to 5-year-old suffer from anemia; a third of children are also underweight [23].

Some major communicable diseases include those which are food and water-borne including diarrhea, hepatitis A and E and typhoid fever. Vector-borne diseases are unequally distributed across the population and consist primarily of dengue fever and malaria. Below is a chart highlighting the access to unimproved water and sanitation services, the major contributors of diarrhea, a condition which kills over 2 million children under five annually in Bangladesh [22] (see **Figure 4**).

Additionally, due to the slums, there is also a high rate of tuberculosis (TB) transmission; Bangladesh ranks within the top 10 globally for TB burden [23]. Obviously, this is unequally distributed across the population, concentrating in poor and uneducated communities.

Noncommunicable diseases include many chronic diseases such as cardiovascular and respiratory diseases, cancer and diabetes. This is dependent on socioeconomic status and literacy due to the etiology of cardiovascular and respiratory diseases/infections (namely COPD, acute lower respiratory infection) due to indoor cook stoves that use biomass for fuel, along with access to healthy foods [24]. Moreover, these numbers are increasing in correlation to the surge in urbanization [23]. The first national study conducted showed roughly 1 in 3 women and 1 in 5 men (age 35 and older) had elevated blood pressure, while about 1in 10 had elevated blood glucose, a biomarker indicating diabetes. Conclusively, cancer is also the sixth leading cause of death [23] (see **Figure 5**).

Because environmental health includes factors determined by not only environmental exposures, but also SES, and therefore political influences and built environment, EH is a multisectoral problem, which requires an equivalently holistic solution [22].

Drinking water source:	**Sanitation facility access:**
improved:	**improved:**
urban: 86.5% of population	urban: 57.7% of population
rural: 87% of population	rural: 62.1% of population
total: 86.9% of population	total: 60.6% of population
unimproved:	**unimproved:**
urban: 13.5% of population	urban: 42.3% of population
rural: 13% of population	rural: 37.9% of population
total: 13.1% of population (2015 est.)	total: 39.4% of population (2015 est.)

Figure 4. Statistics on access to clean water and sanitation facilities in Bangladesh (adapted from https://www.cia.gov/library/publications/the-world-factbook/geos/bg.html).

Environmental burden of disease (preliminary), per year

Estimates based on Comparative Risk Assessment, evidence synthesis and expert evaluation for regional exposure and WHO country health statistics 2004

DALY per 1000 capita preventable through healthier environment

DALYs/1000 cap	(World - lowest: 13, highest: 289)	**64**
Deaths	Deaths preventable through environment each year:	**323 500**
% of total burden		**24%**

Environmental burden by disease category [DALYs/1000 capita], per year

% burden preventable through healthier environments

Disease group	World's lowest country rate	**Country rate**	World's highest country rate
Diarrhoea	0.2	**16**	107
Respiratory infections	0.1	**7.7**	71
Malaria	0.0	**0.6**	34
Other vector-borne diseases	0.0	**1.9**	4.9
Lung cancer	0.0	**0.4**	2.6
Other cancers	0.3	**1.1**	4.1
Neuropsychiatric disorders	1.4	**2.2**	3.0
Cardiovascular disease	1.4	**3.5**	14
COPD	0.0	**1.9**	4.6
Asthma	0.3	**1.3**	2.8
Musculoskeletal diseases	0.5	**0.6**	1.5
Road traffic injuries	0.3	**2.0**	15
Other unintentional injuries	0.6	**7.4**	30
Intentional injuries	0.0	**1.3**	7.5

indicates how preventable environmental burden of disease compares with other countries

indicates how preventable burden of environmental disease is spread across disease groups in the country

Other indicators		
Use of leaded gasoline	No	(2008)
Overcrowding	NA	
Malnutrition (% stunting)	47%	(2006)

Figure 5. Bangladesh environmental burden of disease (adapted from Ref. [6] presentation).

USAID's Country Office for Bangladesh is aimed at building capacity of pertinent government organizations to "reduce environmental health risks through research, policy advice, and awareness raising activities" [24]. The major goals are aimed at addressing (1) indoor air pollution (IAP), (2) occupational health and (3) arsenicosis [24]. IAP and arsenic have become priorities due to the detrimental effects (i.e., neurological impairments, diabetes, hypertension, heart attack and cancer) and exposure distribution. Arsenic is especially concerning due to the fact that it has been identified in shallow tube wells which supply drinking water to communities throughout Bangladesh, many of them rural and poor [25]. Additionally, women and children are disproportionately burdened by IAP due to their extended hours in the household; nearly 92% of the population use solid biomass for fuel, which creates extensive IAP.

Of course environmental health education is an important factor to use in the multisectoral approach also. This effort could educate Bangladeshi people on the importance of understanding arsenic poisoning, indoor air pollution and occupational health exposures which pose health risks. It could also encourage individuals to use cleaner energy sources or if financially limited, well-designed, improved stoves; this would decrease IAP by at least 50% but possibly up to 90% [24]. Occupational exposures are an important factor to consider due to workers' high frequency and magnitude of exposure. This is also important considering the preexisting tension between entrepreneurs and industry—the stigma that compliance and administrative costs deter worker productivity.

WHO Bangladesh worked in collaboration with Bangladeshi personnel to provide training and awareness programs to necessary occupations (i.e., safety officers, inspectors and physicians) [24]. The team also contributed by provided technical support to develop manuals on indoor air pollution, create a national framework for IAP health impact, national strategy for health and safety (in both English and Bangla), and create a data profile of construction sectors on health and safety (base data for construction injury prevalence) and training health care workers to evaluate and treat arsenic-related illnesses. More studies are currently being developed with a focus on occupational health and arsenic exposures and clinical solutions [24].

Other nongovernmental organizations (NGOs) such as the Environment and Social Development Organization (ESDO), are also working toward improving environmental health across Bangladesh. Their main objectives include (1) protecting the environment, (2) reducing poverty, (3) increasing literacy rates and education, (4) empowering woman in rural communities and (5) improving sanitation and health services. Foci are improving livelihoods, SES and environmental education in the most vulnerable parts of Bangladesh [26]. As seen in the multisectoral approach, it is important to have these private-public partnerships, with NGOs building capacity and relationships with community members, increasing success rates.

Notwithstanding all of these efforts, more can certainly be done to combat the burden on environmental health on the population of Bangladesh. Government health expenditures were recorded to be only 2.4% of the GDP in 2014 [21]. Additionally, only less than 62% of the population can read and write, with education expenses being only 2.2% of the GDP [21]. As aforementioned, health disparities plague the country due to SES; these poor literacy rates and minimal government monetary contribution have exacerbated the environmental health exposures and poor health outcomes without a doubt.

Recognizing that the health care system of Bangladesh has gone through a number of changes since their independence in 1971, some great accomplishments and improvements have been made. MDG 4 reducing childhood mortality was achieved before the 2015 target. Additionally, a number of other key indicators have made improvements including TB, diarrhea and malaria [27]. Nonetheless, there are quite a few improvements, which could be made in the current health care system, collaboratively creating the need for a better multisectoral and multipronged approach:

- Better coordination among different ministries implementing primary health care services (both rural and urban areas)
- Need for more health care providers with appropriate skill sets in public sector
- Higher allocation of government budget and less individual out-of-pocket expenses
- Create more equitable access to health care services among rural and urban areas and consistent health financing mechanisms

The current inequitable access to services is the greatest limitation in ensuring universal health care coverage in Bangladesh [27]. As the program currently stands, it is also inadequate in addressing environmental health due to the SES disparity across the country, lack of trained professionals and surveillance of environmental issues, which cause many communicable and noncommunicable diseases along with infrastructure.

7. Sustainability

Firstly, the appropriate approach to integrating EH and UHC must be chosen based on the country's status and needs. All components of this approach must contain clear (SMART) objectives and build collaboration between private and public sectors. Secondly, the approach must be efficient. It has been shown that 20–40% of resources spent on health care are wasted [1]. In implementing universal health care systems, it is imperative to utilize health care services efficiently. This can be addressed in a variety of timeframes—at the "pre" public health community level by educating community members on environmental health exposures and the "post" clinician level, prescribing generic medications and lastly implementing policies, which protect the health of the public [1].

LMIC are notoriously blindsided when it comes to protecting workers' health, especially in terms of child labor and environmental exposures; therefore, public-private partnerships and legislation will be very useful in providing long-term solutions here. Additionally, international efforts to lessen environmental contaminants can be strengthened. This is a much larger issue than EH and UHC, but some of the international topics include global warming and climate change, import and export of goods leading to additional water and air contaminants, global health disparities and inequity in food quality for high- and low-income populations.

The issue of manpower also comes into play when considering the challenges of providing a stable environment for UHCs to flourish. As mentioned previously, intergovernmental agency collaboration and community engagement are vital in EH and UHC in order for the health system and environmental component to work in sync. In order for the EH within UHC to be addressed successfully, programs must provide sustainable solutions to environmental health exposures. The Bangladesh case study proves the need to implement a multipronged and multisectoral approach to ensure success of EH within UHC. Developing relationships through sectors at the regional and local levels would strengthen the likelihood of long-term sustainability after specific programs or projects have ended.

8. Conclusion

As stated by Margaret Chan, Director-General of WHO, "Universal Health Coverage is the single most powerful concept that public health has to offer" [28]. Environmental health must be included within the implementation of a universal health care system due to the high burden of environmentally mediated diseases (~83%) [3]. This further justifies the importance of integrating the two. Despite the multitude of challenges as seen in the Bangladesh case study, there are a wide variety of options to utilize in integrating EH and UHC. By doing so, this ensures people have access to healthy (built) environments and government spending on health care costs associated with many NCDs such as chronic diseases, can be decreased. In LMIC where the burden of disease is highest, the UHC multisectoral approach would be the most beneficial.

Lessons learned from many UHC programs, specifically the Bangladesh case study, include the need for collaboration among sectors, increase in federal health care spending, inclusion of environmental health in UHC and focus on prevention methods. The proper services must also be integrated in order to successfully address health disparities in urban versus rural (or higher versus lower income) areas due to the possible difference in feasibility of service. Opportunities for improvement are plentiful in terms of strengthening the current pilot system through innovative delivery of services, appropriate approaches and implementing policy. As seen in the MDG and SDG, global efforts are being made to address EH and lessen the disease burden, but more can be done at the national policy level as well, especially making more stringent standards.

In conclusion, by implementing country-specific UHC approaches, focusing sufficient government spending on health care (including training health care professionals) and engaging public-private partnerships to successfully target environmental health at the community level, universal health care can be achieved. This would not only create healthier individuals to enter work force and contribute to the economy, while reducing absenteeism, but also reduce poverty by addressing the roots of the problem—the vicious cycle of inequitable health care due to chronic disease and SES.

Appendix A

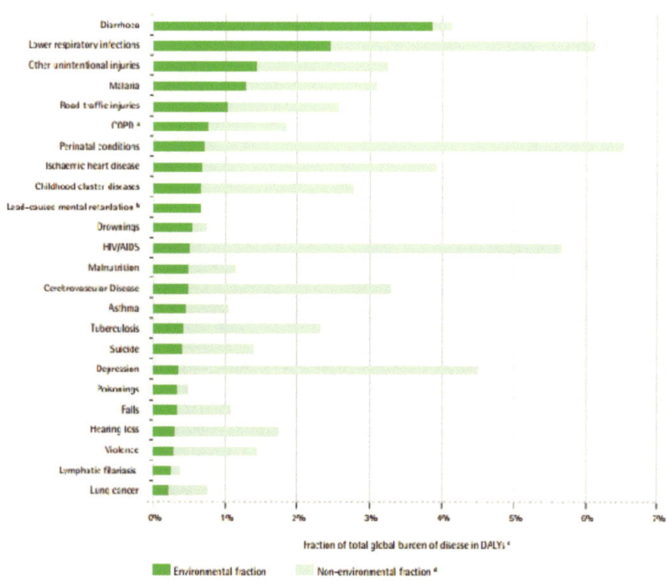

Figure 6. Diseases with the largest environmental contribution (adapted from http://www.who.int/quantifying_ehimpacts/publications/preventingdisease.pdf).

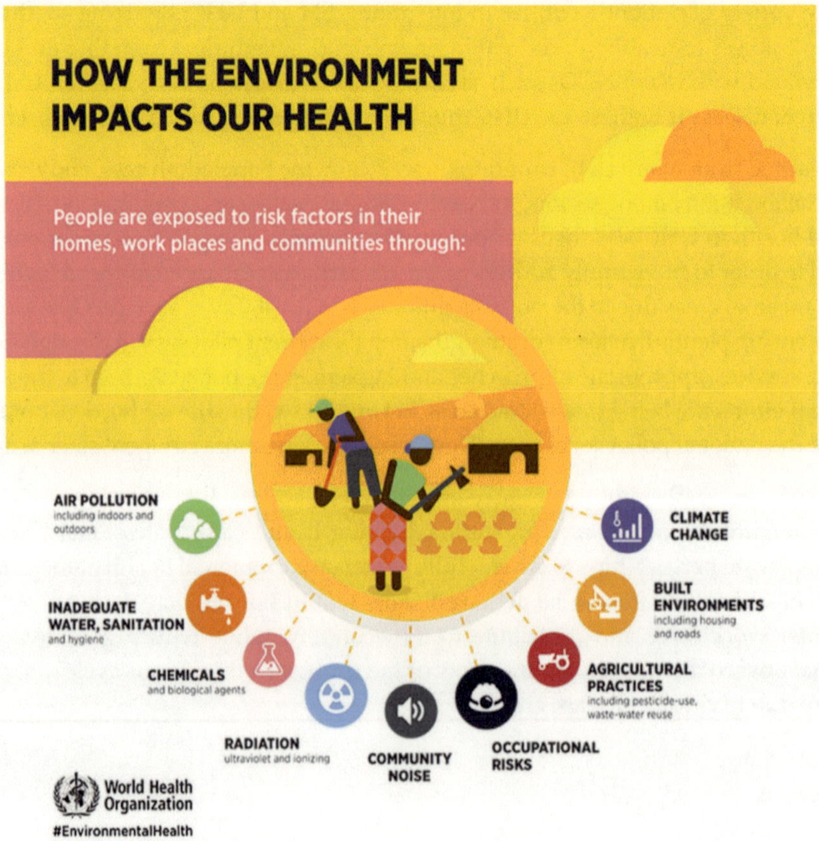

Figure 7. Environmental sources of exposure and impact on health (adapted from http://www.neha.org/about-neha/definitions-environmental-health).

Author details

Muhiuddin Haider* and Katrina Bibb

*Address all correspondence to: mhaider@umd.edu

School of Public Health, Maryland Institute for Applied Environmental Health and Global Health, University of Maryland College Park, College Park, Maryland, USA

References

[1] World Health Organization (WHO). 10 Facts on Universal Health Coverage. 2012. Available from: http://www.who.int/features/factfiles/universal_health_coverage/en/

[2] Chan M, Brundtland GH. Universal Health Coverage: An Affordable Goal for All. Media Centre. 2016. Available from: http://www.who.int/mediacentre/commentaries/2016/universal-health-coverage/en/

[3] Neira M. Health is the Key in Motivating to Solve Environmental Problems. Quantifying Environmental Health Impacts. 2017. Available from: http://www.who.int/quantifying_ehimpacts/publications/previdsvideo/en/

[4] Centers for Disease Control and Prevention (CDC). Global Water, Sanitation, and Hygiene Epidemiology Team. Division of Foodborne, Waterborne, and Environmental Diseases (DFWED). 2014. Available from: https://www.cdc.gov/ncezid/dfwed/waterborne/global.html

[5] World Health Organization (WHO). What is Universal Health Coverage? 2014. Available from: http://www.who.int/features/qa/universal_health_coverage/en/

[6] Haider M, Ahluwalia N. Universal Health Coverage and Environmental Health. 2015

[7] National Environmental Health Association (NEHA). Definitions of Environmental Health. About NEHA. 2017. Available from: http://www.neha.org/about-neha/definitions-environmental-health

[8] Smith KR, Corvalán CF, Kjellström T. How much global ill health is attributable to environmental factors? Epidemiology. 1999;**10**:573-584

[9] World Health Organization (WHO). An Estimated 12.6 Million Deaths Each Year are Attributable to Unhealthy Environments. Media Centre. 2016. Available from: http://www.who.int/mediacentre/news/releases/2016/deaths-attributable-to-unhealthy-environments/en/

[10] World Health Organization (WHO). Noncommunicable Diseases. Media Centre. 2015. Available from: http://www.who.int/mediacentre/factsheets/fs355/en/

[11] Brook RD, et al. Particulate matter air pollution and cardiovascular disease: An update to the scientific statement from the American Heart Association. 2010

[12] Agency for Toxic Substances and Disease Registry (ATSDR). The Priority List of Hazardous Substances that will be the Candidates for Toxicological Profiles. 2016. Available from: https://www.atsdr.cdc.gov/spl/

[13] Agency for Toxic Substances and Disease Registry (ATSDR). Chemicals, Cancer and You. p. 12

[14] World Health Organization (WHO). Flooding and Communicable Diseases Fact Sheet. Humanitarian Health Action. Available from: http://www.who.int/hac/techguidance/ems/flood_cds/en/

[15] Prüss-Üstün A, Corvalán C. Preventing Disease through Healthy Environments. World Health Organization (WHO); 2006. p. 106

[16] World Health Organization (WHO). Health, Environment and the Millennium Development Goals (MDGs). Environment and Health in Developing Countries. 2017. Available from: http://www.who.int/heli/risks/ehindevcoun/en/index2.html

[17] Alsan M, Westerhaus M, Herce M, Nakashima K, Farmer P. Poverty, global health and infectious disease: Lessons from Haiti and Rwanda. Infectious Disease Clinics of North America. 2011;**25**:611-622

[18] Gustafsson-Wright E, Schellekens O. Achieving Universal Health Coverage in Nigeria One State at a Time: A Public-Private Partnership Community-Based Health Insurance Model. 2013

[19] Maeda A, et al. Universal Health Coverage for Inclusive and Sustainable Development: A Synthesis of 11 Country Case Studies. The World Bank; 2014. p. 75

[20] World Health Organization (WHO). Household Air Pollution and Health. Media Centre. 2016. Available from: http://www.who.int/mediacentre/factsheets/fs292/en/

[21] USA Central Intelligence Agency (CIA). South Asia: Bangladesh. The World Factbook. 2015. Available from: https://www.cia.gov/library/publications/the-world-factbook/geos/bg.html

[22] Hossain MA, Moniruzzaman M, Islam MA. Urban environmental health in Bangladesh slum: A comparative study of two metropolitan cities. 2010;**8**(1-2):67-76

[23] United States Agency for International Development (USAID). Chapter Three: Major Public Health Issues in Bangladesh. Available from: https://www.k4health.org/toolkits/bangladesh-health-journalists/overview-health-bangladesh#block-views-toolkit-page-resources-block

[24] WHO Bangladesh. Environmental and Occupational Health. 2017. Available from: http://www.searo.who.int/bangladesh/areas/environmentandoccupationalhealth/en/

[25] Human Rights Watch. Bangladesh: 20 Million Drink Arsenic-Laced Water 20 Years After Discovery, Failing Government Response. 2016. Available from: https://www.hrw.org/news/2016/04/06/bangladesh-20-million-drink-arsenic-laced-water

[26] Environment and Social Development Organization (ESDO). Environmental Health. 2017. Available from: http://esdo.org/environmental-health/

[27] World Health Organization (WHO). Bangladesh Health System Review. Asia Pacific Observatory on Health Systems and Policies; 2015. p. 214

[28] World Health Organization (WHO). Health Research is Essential for Progress Towards Universal Health Coverage. Media Centre. 2013. Available from: http://www.who.int/mediacentre/news/releases/2013/world_health_report_20130815/en/